Life Bet
Mountains and the Sea

A Memoir of an Irish Childhood

Mary M. Trant

ISBN:

Paperback: 978-1-0686027-1-9

E-Book 978-1-0686027-0-2

This book is a work of fiction based on real events. Names, characters, places and incidents are either a product of the author's imagination or are used fictitiously. Any resemblance to actual people, living or dead, events or locales is entirely coincidental.

First published in Ireland by Mary M. Trant in 2024.

Printed in the United Kingdom.

Dedication

In loving memory of my parents and grandparents.

My endless gratitude to my husband David and my family Linda, Paul, Jack, Eleanor, Eamon and Billy for your support and encouragement.

For my long-departed donkey Neddy, I forgive you for throwing me in the briars and nettles – there is no glory in trying to outsmart a donkey!

Table of Contents

Maggie and Ted

Having pondered for way too long, I am excited to recount my childhood adventures, most of which I shared with my brother Ted, and how our lives were influenced by family members and where we lived in rural Ireland.

My brother, Ted, born in 1950, was now seven years old – a big burly lad, with curly red hair that leaped around his head like springs. I, Maggie, was one year his junior, slight in stature, with rosy-red cheeks, and silky black hair.

In our childhood years we were blessed to be surrounded by Kate, our mum, and Jimmy, our pop. This blessing was twofold, with Nano and Grandpa John, our paternal grandparents, also living with us. We had two older sisters, Cait and Elizabeth, but it was a foregone conclusion that Ted and I would be playmates, as we were nearest in age.

At this time, the Irish language was still used by our parents and grandparents, albeit sparingly and intermingled with English. We lived in the most picturesque part of Ireland, between the mountains and sea, in a wee townland called Gorse Valley in County Kerry. The mountain range above our farm holding, and the sea below, stretched for miles in either direction – a townland of rugged magical beauty and a neigh-bourhood where everyone supported each other.

I invite you to come back with me, to where we had time to be children and life moved at a slower pace. Enjoy the journey!

Maggie – 2024

Homestead

Once the clock struck six each morning, life on our homestead was a flurry of activity. Family and farm life for Ted and I was a most wonderous time, with each day lived to the full.

Mum was the powerhouse behind all activity in our home, and she also did many farm chores on a daily basis. I loved to hear her sing while she ambled around our kitchen, wearing a black and white flowery dress, her favourite clothing item. Our beautiful mum had curly black hair, bright sparkling eyes, and sallow skin.

Our father was better known to us as Pop. He was sharp featured, tall and lean, and a worldly-wise man. When working on our farm, his usual attire was brown tweed trousers, a handknitted jumper, and a check flat cap with a small stiff brim, turned sideways on his head. He worked hard to support our family but was not even-tempered. Indeed, I remember him as a timebomb that could explode given the slightest provocation.

Cait and Elizabeth, being older, often lost their patience with Ted and me, as we were giddy goats. Cait, the eldest, was the bossy one. Sometimes we would sneak into the kitchen and help ourselves to some bullseye sweets stored in a tin, without permission. The ever-vigilant Cait would make a hullabaloo about it.

"Hey, you two, I'm going to tell Mum that you took sweets."

"Aw, Cait, we are really sorry, please don't tell Mum," I would plead with her in the hope she would forget. But, like an elephant, she never did.

Cait most always sported a cheeky grin. She loved to wear a skirt and V-neck jumper, and always tied her long hair back in a ponytail. Elizabeth was more ladylike, with short black bobbed hair, and she loved to wear a plain-colour dress.

Heavenly aromas filled the air in Gorse Valley during springtime and early summer when honeysuckle, rhododendrons, fuchsia, foxglove, and yellow gorse flowered.

Twittering swallows arrived in droves in early April and busied themselves building their nests in the barns and sheds. Soon, Ted and I would watch the gearrcachs – baby birds – peep from their hideaway buried in the eaves of our outhouses. We used to climb up to see them, ugly, hairy, and purple-skinned, with their beaks opened wide, thinking it was Mama bird coming with food. Sadly, a chick was often splattered on the ground, its mother having thrown its lifeless body out of the nest after it lost its battle for survival.

Cuckoos echoed from distant vales, and corncrakes called to each other from hay meadows on long, humid summer evenings.

Our two-storey home was situated back a little from a winding stone-walled road. To one side of it, a boreen – a narrow little road with a grassy centre – had an abundance of flora and fauna dancing alongside it. Beginning at the hillside, it stretched down to the sea, with a river flowing along its length, slipping under a quaint bridge across the roadway.

The house was built in the early nineteen twenties with the help of neighbours and a government grant. Our kitchen, which also served as our living space, was sparsely furnished. A wooden chair with a straw rope seat – a súgán chair – sat at one side of the open-hearth fire, and a wooden bench provided a family seating area at the other. Chairs and a bulky wooden kitchen table rested underneath a net-curtain-clad front window, and, on the opposite side, a box radio sat on a small table under the back window. Beneath the stairs, nook shelves held pots, pans, our galvanised wash tub, and other kitchen accoutrements. We had electricity for lights only and our radio was battery operated.

Our home's only source of heat was the open fireplace in the kitchen, which was also used for airing, drying clothes and cooking. Our mum insisted that all clothes should be bone dry before being worn by any family member. She feared if they weren't so, we would catch a cold, flu, or some worse illness.

She often said, "Don't put on that garment, you'll catch your death of pneumonia." And to be sure, she made us wear vests.

During wintertime, the grand parlour room was cold, as were the bedrooms upstairs. Overcoats served as extra blankets during the bitterest months. If I were crying in bed at night during this time of year, Mum would come up the stairs and say, "What's wrong, Maggie? Are you cold?"

"I'm not just cold, Mum, my feet are like ice blocks."

She would throw a heavy coat over my blankets, and with its extra weight bearing down on me, I would sleep like a newborn baby.

Back then, we ate whatever the adults in our house had for their meals, but in smaller quantities. Potatoes, homemade bread, porridge, carrots, bacon and cabbage were our staple foods. Sometimes we had a guggy egg – a boiled egg mashed up in a cup, with lashings of butter and some salt. But we did not eat boiled crubeens – pigs' feet – which were delicacies that only Pop loved. All of our food was cooked in big black pots suspended from a crane – a black cast iron device which hung over the open fire and could be lowered or raised from the heat.

When we weren't feeling well, 'Goody' – bread mashed in a mug of hot milk and sugar – was never refused. Custard and jelly after Sunday dinner was my favourite of all.

A veritable zoo of farm animals lived in our back yard. Our cows sheltered and were milked in an old whitewashed thatched cottage – once the home of my great-grandparents.

We also had a corrugated iron roof calf shed and pigsty. Our equines had their own stone-built stable, with a hay barn close by. Not forgetting Mum's hens, her pride and joy, who resided in an old tumbledown stone-built shed, with a rusty, leaking tin roof, though they had laying boxes aplenty.

The donkey cart and pony trap, including the turf, were stored in an open, tin-roofed lean-to shed. Shovels, spades, and many other small farm implements were stored in this shed, including bunches of onions, which hung from the wooden rafters.

Our farm holding was the source of most of our food. The cows provided milk and butter, while cabbage and onions were homegrown in a plot at the side of the house. A small amount of early potatoes were sown in wide ridges here too, which were ready for consumption when all of last year's crop had been depleted in July. Grandpa's calloused hands were evidence of how he carefully tended to our vegetable garden during the growing season. He hoed the weeds and dug in rotted farmyard manure with a four-prong pike where needed. Day after day, he painstakingly broke up clods of earth into finer soil with a spade and covered the vegetables with it. After his crops ripened, I watched how he proudly presented them to Mum and Nano in the kitchen, to cook for dinner.

Our hens delivered eggs on a daily basis, and the nearby ocean offered up a bountiful supply of fresh fish. In a field a short distance away, our main crop of potatoes grew and pro-

vided us with a beautiful harvest of dry flowery 'Kerr Pinks'
– Mum's favourite spud.

We had a yard at the back of our house called a haggard,
which was a play area for our animals, intermingled with us,
their human family, and a plethora of farming equipment and
scattered straw. Here, an abundance of what I thought were
onions grew in a grassy patch in one corner. I once picked a
bunch and brought them into Mum in the kitchen.

"Mum, here are some onions to cook for dinner."

"Maggie, they are not onions, darling, they are daffodils.
But it's easy to mistake them because they have green leaves
and bulbs like onions."

Singing in soprano mode, Mum placed the daffodil bunch
in an old white enamel jug of water and displayed them on
the kitchen windowsill. Always kind, Mum did this so I
wouldn't feel disheartened.

Even though it pains me to mention it, we killed a pig,
which was preserved with salt, then hung from the shed's
rafters. It lasted for months and was a sight I found difficult
to look at.

My brother and I loved to sneak down the boreen adja-
cent to our home, to the strand when the tide had gone out. I
can vividly remember it being like an artist's creation, where
we left our footprints in the shimmering swathes of wet sand,
dipped our feet in the warm pools of seawater, and inhaled
the salty scent of the ocean.

The shoreline was alive with barnacled rocks, cockles,
mussels, and much more. We could pass an hour or so frol-
icking in its midst, with shrieking flocks of seagulls our only
company, and if we got hungry, we had shellfish to sustain us.
Rocks were aplenty, and handy tools for breaking the shells. I
remember the woody odour of seaweed was ever-present.

As children who lived close by the sea, my brother and I had a natural and healthy respect for it. We learned of its dangers from an early age from Mum, Nano, and Grandpa. When the frothy waves were creeping towards us, we knew it was time to return home.

Sometimes, our parents and grandparents grumbled about the incessant lashing rain and gale-force winds sweeping in from the Atlantic Ocean, or the mist from the mountains engulfing our homestead in wintertime, making farm life difficult. But to me, it was always summer between the mountains and sea in Gorse Valley – a place where Ted and I were free to be children and grow up at our own pace, in peace and quiet, and always close to nature.

Nano

My big brother and I were blessed that we shared our home and family life with Nano and Grandpa, our dad's wonderful parents. Nano was a pure lady, with silver hair tied back in a bun and she loved to wear black clothing. She was an amazing cook, and we loved Fridays when she prepared a fish dish for our family dinner. Her freshly caught ling fish, served with homemade white sauce, was delicious.

Nano made wonderful white soda bread daily. She did not need a recipe for this amazing bread, as she had the measurements in her head – a little scoop of this and a wee pinch of that. Before kneading the bread with her gentle touch, she floured her hands for what was pure poetry in motion. She baked it in a big black cast-iron pot, hung from the crane over the open fire. Sitting on a chair beside the fire, she watched that bread like a hawk, turning it over several times to make sure it was baked evenly on each side. I loved to run into our kitchen and smell the aroma of her freshly baked bread.

In the early 1920s and before Nano married Grandpa, she dwelled in unusual living accommodation. Her home had whitewashed walls, with a red corrugated iron roof. The cottage boasted a bright-red door and two windows. Her idyllic wee townland consisted of a cluster of six identical cottages built in a half circle, and all the inhabitants were related to each other. To the front lay a natural pond, in which ducks quacked and swam surrounded by a plethora of golden daffodils in early spring.

Nano often put her arms around Ted and me, sitting by the fire before bedtime in our home, and told us stories about where she lived. One story I particularly remember was about the settle bed. It was a natural wooden four-seater-style bench, placed beside the open-hearth fire in their living room. As their home had only one bedroom, it was necessary for some family members to sleep on the settle bed. At night, the seat area of the bench was unfolded down to reveal a mattress. Nano and her two older sisters snuggled together and slept on this, the settle bed.

So quaint was her beautiful home and surroundings, you could never imagine anyone leaving this peaceful place. But leave it Nano did at seventeen years of age, to work in the big houses of the gentry, and she told my brother and me many stories about her employers.

Domestic service was one of the few jobs open to girls back then. To begin with, Nano was employed as an assistant cook and cleaner for the lords and ladies of these magnificent stately homes, who entertained royally and gardened loftily. In return, she was offered lodgings in the meagre servant quarters of the grand houses, as well as a subsistence wage.

The lady of the big house, the epitome of elegance in her flowing gown, spent much of her time in the grand garden, with the head gardener taking care of her every need. Once the sun was high, she could be seen sitting at her white cast-iron outdoor dining set, reading a novel and sipping fine wine.

During the day, the lord of the manor wore a jacket and waistcoat over knickerbockers. They were laced at the knee, complemented by woollen knee-high socks. He wore a bowler hat, smoked a finely curved pipe, and always carried an amber-coloured cane with a shepherd's crook at the top. During the day, he passed his time in the estate, fishing and game shooting, with the assistance of his head gamekeeper.

In the evenings, the lord and lady entertained gentry in the grand parlour of their mansion and sometimes even royalty. These guests mostly came from similar grand mansions in the surrounding countryside and travelled in style in magnificent four-wheeled carriages guided by an impeccably dressed coachman and pulled by meticulously groomed black horses with feather plumes between their ears, their harnesses gleaming in the brightly lit cobbled drive and courtyard.

The parlour room was decorated with flowers of every description, chosen and picked fresh from the garden. A multitude of fine silver platters and floral gilt-edged delftware decorated a lavish mahogany table in the middle of the room. No more than twelve guests were seated at any one time on the matching carved mahogany chairs, to ensure they could converse with each other at ease.

Their banquet consisted of homemade onion soup for starters, roast pheasant and vegetable dish for dinner, followed by dessert of various puddings, and finished off with a cheese board, tea, and biscuits. The guests then retired to the grand sitting room and played card games, with smoking and drinking aplenty.

But there were some other little perks to Nano's employment in the big houses. From the upper-class way of life of these folks, she learned valuable lessons in ladylike etiquette, which she retained throughout her life.

During her work, going from one big house to the next, she learned a huge amount of geography and was deeply knowledgeable about the county she lived in. She knew every village and townland for miles around. I can still recall, if anyone in the neighbourhood was looking for the whereabouts of a particular town, all they had to do was ask Nano and, hey presto, she had the exact location, quicker than the modern-day Google Maps.

In late August or early September, when the bushes in the boreen were heavy with blackberries, Ted and I helped Nano pick a large volume of scrumptious fruits provided by nature, filling three or four shiny one-gallon sweet tin cans to over-flowing. As enthusiastic as we were, Nano always reminded us to leave some berries for the birds.

Back home, she would wash the berries several times, to re-move any creepy crawlies who may have made a home in them. The blackberries were then simmered, and when they were soft enough, she added the perfect amount of sugar to sweeten them before mashing the mixture to a pulp. I loved to help her fill sterilised jam jars full of the rich purple mixture.

For many weeks afterwards, we had blackberry jam aplen-ty to put on buttered bread. I have tried for many years to repeat Nano's recipe for homemade blackberry jam but have always failed to perfect that nose-tingling aroma and lip-smacking taste she could create blindfolded.

Nano

A lovable Lady, so very fair,
With glittery, gleaming silver hair.
Always the kindest, always the best,
Yet too often too slow to rest.
You have been at peace for a while,
Wings and a halo always in style.
Your memory is a blessing, sweet Nano,
I praise your love as I sing from below.

– Maggie –

Grandpa

Grandpa John was a tall, raw-boned man, who wore an old black suit, with a pinstripe collarless shirt. He also wore a fedora-style hat, which he tipped to one side when greeting ladies, priests, or gardaí – policemen.

Underneath his attire in wintertime, he wore a pair of cream-coloured long johns to keep nice and warm. I remember that during this time of year, he also liked to wear a Fair Isle woollen jumper, which he called his gansey.

He regularly listened to the Seanchaí – a storyteller – in the late evening when all farm chores were done. Grandpa's mood lifted when he listened to the Seanchaí, but that man's voice grated on my nerves. I just couldn't listen to him. I often asked my grandfather to turn off the radio and he always replied with, "Hould your whist, Maggie. He'll be finished in a few minutes."

I would sigh. "Okay, okay, Grandpa."

One particular day, I embarrassed Grandpa John more than he ever wanted to remember. A pension officer called by our home with a stack of forms held in a folder under his oxter – armpit. These forms were for Grandpa to complete, and maybe divulge information he did not want any government department to gain knowledge of. This officer was the last man on earth he wanted to meet.

At that time, I was sitting on the bottom step of our stairs, right next to the front door. The officer knocked on our door, rather loudly in my estimation.

"Grandpa, Grandpa, he'll break down our door."

My grandfather put his hand over my mouth and whispered in my ear, "Shush, shush, Maggie. You'll get me hung." His way of saying I would get him into big trouble.

I did shush, until the pension officer knocked again. This time I repeated the same outburst, but louder. Grandpa scampered out the back door and left Nano in charge of the situation. The dilemma ended well, as the pension officer didn't gain entrance to our house that day.

Grandpa smoked a *dúdín* – a mahogany-coloured brown pipe, with a black stem or mouthpiece, made of hardened clay – and I remember him giving it a tap on the palm of his hand to remove any old residual tobacco before having his next puff. He used a cube of Watchman's tobacco, which he shaved slices from with the small blade of his penknife. With the tobacco held in the palm of his calloused hand, he would use the knuckles of his other hand to crush it into smithereens before filling his pipe.

Sitting back on his *súgán* chair beside the fire, as if he had all the time in the world, he'd take long inhales or puffs of his *dúdín*, like a child sucking a favourite lollipop. He spent a huge amount of time trying to keep it lighting, striking one matchstick after another and poking and prodding the contents of its bowl with his forefinger. Feathery plumes of smoke filled the kitchen, and while I wasn't a huge fan of tobacco fumes, almost fifty years later, I still have that penknife packed away safe in a box in remembrance of him.

Whilst puffing his pipe, he told Ted and me stories about the troubled times in our townland and surrounding areas, which appeared to have affected him deeply. I recall him repeating the stories many times.

Long before I was born, during the early 1920s, Ireland was not a free country, its people forced to live under the influence of an occupying military force. Grandpa and likeminded people were endeavouring to change the situation, so the citizens of this country, and in particular those in Gorse Valley, could determine their own future.

When Grandpa was nearing his twentieth year, life changed dramatically. He had to leave his ailing parents with the farm workload and go live in a stone-built dugout on the side of the mountain with his comrades, going on to fight with every ounce of strength to defend what was rightfully theirs.

Grandpa mentioned a road blockade to stop the advance of the occupiers, which my brother and I later learned was an ambush. He also mentioned that on one occasion he walked back through the rough mountain terrain, in the dead of night, and knocked on the door of a neighbouring family to tell them heartbreaking news about their son. Tears trickled down his face as he told us this.

I remember him telling us about a kind woman who brought food to their dugout. She trudged through the mountainous area in the dark of night, with heavy bags of food for as long as was necessary, to make sure they didn't go hungry.

Grandpa was always incredibly careful not to divulge details of the troubles that were unfit for Ted and me to hear. But, in later years, I learned more about these dreadful times in Ireland, especially about more local atrocities. I also realised that it was possible that Grandpa was suffering from Post Traumatic Stress Disorder, which would explain his sadness and the need to repeat the stories over and over again.

When the occupation ended in 1922, with the rebels having gained independence for part of the country, the community of Gorse Valley thought they could rebuild their lives. But no, the ensuing Civil War brought equal, if not more trouble and despair into 1923.

Civil War

The Civil War of 1922 and 1923 was a conflict between Irish Nationalists regarding the issue of whether or not to accept the Anglo-Irish Treaty, reached when the occupiers and the Irish negotiators established that twenty-six of the thirty-two counties became the Irish Free State, and which ended the Irish War of Independence.

The Civil War, one of atrocity and bloodshed, arose between those in favour of and those against the Treaty. It was so divisive that, in some instances, it put members of the same family on opposite sides, as there was no middle ground, leaving brother fighting brother and father fighting son. Also, friend fought with friend and neighbour turned against neighbour.

The impact of the Irish Civil War was enormous and deeply affected those involved. Many survivors emigrated, and those who remained struggled to return to normal life, suffering with mental health problems or alcohol addiction. This led to tough times in Gorse Valley, as County Kerry and other southern counties were particularly affected by the conflict.

Eventually, in May 1923, a ceasefire and an order to dump arms was called, effectively ending the Civil War. The aftermath of these troubled times left destitution in their wake for Grandpa, his parents, and the surrounding communities.

In Gorse Valley, back then, the people had little or nothing. Electricity was unavailable, water on tap an unattainable aspiration, and most hadn't time to indulge in dreams. Every day of the week, fifty-two weeks of the year, was a struggle to survive.

I recall Grandpa often mentioning that the chilly winds that blew in from the raging sea, the mist from the mountains and deluges of rain that enveloped the valley in wintertime added to the hardship endured back then.

They got up at the crack of dawn, with their few cows needing to be milked twice a day, every day. The cowshed had to be cleaned out of cow dung – cow excrement. Afterwards, sops – small bundles of straw bedding for the cows – were spread out in the shed daily. Water was got from the nearby wells and carried to the animals, and fodder was dragged wherever it was needed. Hay and oats had to be cut by hand if the weather was benevolent, and dry-stone walls needed repair after the ravages of winter. A cow or two had to be attended to while calving, and the same applied to sows giving birth to their piglets. These latter events, more often than not, took place in the middle of the night. Regardless, having had little or no sleep, the farmers had to be up early the next morning to begin another day's work. Donkeys had to be harnessed to bring the milk to the creamery, with horses also harnessed to plough the fields. And drains needed to be dug to keep the fields from flooding. The list was endless.

I remember in later years a story Grandpa told Ted and me, about a local man he knew quite well. The man was sent to the workhouse for being homeless. He had tried to keep himself fed by stealing potatoes, and while he was in the workhouse, he attempted to burn the place down. People said that the workhouse was worse than prison but he had done nothing, really; his real crime was poverty.

As a child looking out the window of our home, at the magical beauty of Gorse Valley, it was hard for me to comprehend that it was not always an idyllic place to live. Grandpa looking out the same window, eyes tearing up, was testament that he experienced a completely different view of the valley: a battle ground, with horrific memories forever etched in his mind. I often wished that I could have cheered him up in some way during his reflective times.

The purpose of the fight for independence was that our family and families in our community could have a better future, though many suffered during that time and in the aftermath.

Living in London

Pop aspired to better himself and improve our family's living standards. He could have been a fisherman, a construction labourer, or continued trying to eke out a living from our farm, but he chose a different career path.

Opportunity to better oneself in Gorse Valley was non-existent because it had not recovered from the Irish War of Independence and the ensuing Civil War of the early 1920s. Industry was lacking, work was scarce, and farms were small. Raising a family from the income of a small farm was not sustainable.

Pop's brother, our uncle Peter, was already living in London. He often told Mum and Pop how wonderful life was in this great city and they eventually decided that we would go there and start a new life. At that time, Cait was four years old, Elizabeth was three and Ted was a toddler. I was a five-month-old baby and obviously I have no memory of living in London. But stories of our time spent there was a topic of conversation within our family for many years into the future.

Having said a heartbreaking goodbye to Nano and Grandpa, our young family left Gorse Valley and emigrated to London, travelling there by ship. While we were there, Nano and Grandpa took care of the farm, a task they were young enough to manage at that time.

Pop was in his twenty-fourth year, and his face lit up with a smile when he was offered a carpentry apprenticeship with a construction company. Uncle Peter was instrumental in helping him find this job.

Having the might of a lion, he spent his working days cutting, shaping, and hammering the finest wood into masterpieces. With his chin held high with pride, everything he had been hoping for and dreaming of was coming through. His face beamed with delight when, after two years, he received his Master Carpentry Craftsman Certification.

Coming from a small townland in rural Ireland, adjusting to living in London was a tough undertaking for Pop and Mum, especially with four young children. While there were opportunities to better oneself, it was a city of hustle and bustle, and Pop and Mum had to immerse themselves in strange cultures and a faster rhythm of life.

They persevered for a while, with Pop working hard in the construction company and Mum trying to keep us children occupied throughout the day in a small flat. She took us for long walks in a nearby park, where we had fun on swings and slides, and she did the grocery shopping, not easy with us in tow. Back in our lodgings, we played with toys, did some colouring and Mum told us stories. Cait always recalled a walkie-talkie doll she played with and Ted had his first introduction to diecast aeroplanes, which fascinated him for many years afterwards.

We spent the weekends with our uncle Peter and his family, sightseeing and doing some clothes shopping. Mum often recalled the wonderful shops she went into and bought beautiful quality wool. She knitted cardigans and jumpers from the woollen hanks for us children any spare moment she could.

Cait attended kindergarten for some hours during weekdays, close to where we lived. To say she didn't like it would be an understatement. It was complicated by the fact she was amongst cockney children, who found it difficult to understand her thick Kerry accent.

Even though we were getting along, Mum and Pop missed their relatives, including friends and longed for our home and traditional way of life in Gorse Valley. As a result, our time in London was short-lived. Once Pop had finished his two-year apprenticeship a decision was made, and we returned to our homestead. But I do remember him being forever grateful for his apprenticeship and associated work in the city of London.

Mass and Prayers

During late evening time, when all chores were done, our family sat together and told stories beside the fire. Our big black cast-iron kettle was forever singing on the crane over the fire, providing boiling water for tea.

Some evenings, Ted and I would mount our imaginary mustangs – sweeping brushes – and gallop around and around the concrete floor of our kitchen, holding the wooden handle of the brush with one hand and slapping our hips with the other, willing our mounts to go faster. Our family thought our horse show was great fun.

At nine o'clock sharp, the old mahogany box radio was turned on for news of the day. If any child made as much as a squeak while the newsreader broadcast mostly unwelcome news, they were shushed by an adult, or maybe two adults in unison. For some reason, this was the time that the two of us went into full flight, chattering and giggling.

Mum, with her head between her hands on the table, exhausted after her hard day's work, would often say, "Ted and Maggie, will you two shush? You have my head in a bodhran."

Her outbursts were twofold: to try and save her sanity, and to protect us from the caustic tongue of our father. Still, it was funny to think of us having her head in a drum.

On other occasions, if there was a Gaelic football match being broadcast on this state-of-the-art 1950s boombox radio, it would have been easier for Ted and me to go live in the cowshed. If we opened our mouths during the game, both our father and grandfather would create a scene. During these unnerving matches, Grandpa and Pop had sweat pouring from their brows, their faces turned red as a turkey cock's waffle, willing on their county team. It was so important to them that Kerry won, the tension of the match risked one of them to have a heart attack at any given time.

Once the adults were suitably depressed by the late evening news, the radio was switched off and Nano would announce it was time for the rosary. We all knelt by a chair and the rosary beads went into action. Nano led the first mystery, Grandpa the second, Mum the third, and Pop the fourth. By the time it came to Cait or Elizabeth's turn to lead the fifth mystery, my big brother and I were so weary of the litany of prayers, it wasn't unusual to find us slumped over a chair, fast asleep.

But the prayers didn't finish with the fifth mystery. Our grandmother would continue with the Hail Holy Queen, the never-ending litany of the Blessed Virgin, and prayers for the living and the dead. She continued, asking Saint Paul, Saint Peter, Jesus, Mary, and Holy Saint Joseph to help and protect us, ending with, "Thank you, Dear Lord, for everything you have bestowed upon this family today."

I once heard Cait and Elizabeth whisper to each other in sheer disbelief, wondering what on earth Nano was talking about – our family had absolutely nothing bestowed upon us this day. Mum gave them one of her sidelong glances, and they put their hands together, looking up to Heaven, as if they were angels, hoping the prayer ritual had at last ended. The amazing thing is, I hear myself say similar prayers nowadays, to protect my family.

Sometimes Ted got confused blessing himself – making the Sign of the Cross – using his left hand instead of his right, as he was inclined to be a *ciotóg* – of left-handed dominance. A huff and puff would come from the other side of the kitchen, and on peering across, Pop had a scowl on his face. Ted's unintentional mistake always irritated the living daylights out of him because he did not want any son of his being a *ciotóg*. I would move in front of my brother, take his hands in mine and show him the correct way to bless himself. Surely that is what Pop should have done, and I returned the angry scowl right back at him in annoyance for upsetting Ted. Even though I was only six years old, I distinctly remember thinking how Pop's harsh attitude towards Ted on these occasions proved that his devout prayers were doing little to spiritually transform him.

On Saturday night, the activity in our kitchen amped up big time. Mum prepared as if we were going to meet the good man above himself, though we were just going to Mass the next day. Out came the large, galvanised tin bath, about three foot in length, with sixteen-inch sides and a handle at each end. It had many uses in our household: washing clothes, the legs of kitchen chairs; a carrier for potatoes and apples; or for holding rainwater. But on Saturday evening it was used for scrubbing a week's worth of farm mud from our sun-kissed bodies. Particularly so for Ted and me, as we were outdoor children.

Mum stoked up a blazing turf fire and the bath was placed in front of it. Our black cast-iron kettle was boiled several times on the crane over the fire and added to the half-full bath of chilly water. Lifebuoy – strong-smelling carbolic soap – and a facecloth were put to the test washing each child dunked in the tub.

"Maggie, you go first, sweetheart," Mum would say, as I was the youngest. Luckily for me, as then it was Ted's turn, followed by Elizabeth, and lastly Cait, without even a change of fresh water.

Once our baths were over and done with, Mum would brush our hair straight. Sometimes she'd run an ivory flea comb through it, to make sure any foreign invaders were not residing on our scalps. There were no magical lice-killer lotions available when I was a child.

If our hair needed to be cut, Pop took care of that, with military precision. Out came the sharp-as-a-tack shiny silver scissors that he alone was allowed to use. When he'd finished clipping my hair it looked like he had used a breakfast bowl on my head to guide his large rough and weatherbeaten hands. Luckily, it never took too long for my hair to grow back.

To her horror, Elizabeth got the same bowl hair style as I did, but for the most part Cait escaped our artistic barber, as her hair was long and tied back.

"Maggie, I don't want Pop to cut my hair," Ted whispered.

"Oh, Ted, I know, I know. But why don't you just let him? It will be easier and cause less fuss."

"Okay," he replied with trepidation.

With Ted having red bushy hair, it took longer for Pop to manoeuvre the scissors around his head. I stood close by my brother and watched him cringe as Pop's face flushed red and his patience waned, resulting in a rather short back-and-sides hairstyle for his son.

Donned in our pyjamas, we'd go off to bed, where Mum tucked us in, told us a story, and, as always before she left our room, assured us that our guardian angel would protect us during the night.

Grandpa prepared the pony trap for our Sunday-morning travels by polishing and shining it the evening before. He lubricated its wheels and axle with goose grease. A state-of-the-art mahogany trap with bright red wheels and shafts, it had an under-sprung carriage for comfort of travel on the rough, bumpy roads. Bright-red cushions adorned the seats, and the back door had a shiny brass handle. A black iron step just below the door made it easy to climb into.

Our pony, Blackie, who pulled the trap to Mass, also got a makeover from Grandpa. She was chubby and as black as soot, hence her name. Though small in stature, she was hardy, and had unrelenting determination. Typical of the Kerry Bog Pony breed, she had a fine intelligent head, and between her ears, her mane grew in mohawk style. She had what seemed like an angry face but was an adorable pony, with no anger traits whatsoever. In preparation for Sunday morning, Grandpa brushed her coat and trimmed her mane and tail. He also cleaned her tackle, and when he'd finished, the leather was soft and supple, the brass buckles glistening in the slanting evening sun.

At that stage, peace reigned. Mum made the smouldering fire safe, but the little lamp under the large Sacred Heart picture on the wall always remained lit. All was quiet in our small kitchen, except for the ticking of the clock on the mantlepiece. We could sleep in our cosy beds, ready for the next morning.

When Sunday arrived, Grandpa dressed in a black suit, white shirt, and hat. He yoked the pony to the trap, took his position upfront, and off we'd go to Mass. Mum put large bows in Cait, Elizabeth's, and my hair, matching our beautiful red coats. But I pulled mine off, as it was annoying me, and hid it in my pocket. Ted wore short tweed pants, knee-high socks, and an Aran jumper. Mum and Nano were dressed like queens. Pop cycled behind us, as only seven of us could squeeze into the trap. He dressed in a stylish shirt and jacket, and always wore bicycle clips around the bottom of his trouser legs, to prevent black greasy oil from the chain staining them. On appearance, you would think butter wouldn't melt in his mouth.

Grandpa commanded the pony to "Hup now, girl", a signal she understood well to begin the journey to the church a few townlands away, and she quickened to an even trot. As we got nearer the church, she would falter from the pressure of pulling the trap, with seven of us onboard, with foamy white sweat lathering her rump and thighs. Grandpa tied her to a rusty iron hook outside the church wall, alongside many other horses and ponies with traps, who had completed a similar journey for their respective owners. He knew she would cool down and be rested for the return journey home after Mass was finished.

While the reverent congregation in the church offered up prayers, there were always some hesitant characters standing outside the door chatting. The main part of the Mass was said in Latin, and most children hadn't the slightest clue what the priest was saying, or the response required. But we imitated a mumbo jumbo of words, which sounded good at the time.

When the priest had finished his lengthy sermon about the eighth commandment, 'Thou Shalt Not Steal', and finished banging his fist off the pulpit, the sense of relief was palpable, particularly so from the children, as they thought the service had finished. But no, the singing of the hymns *Adeste Fideles* or the *Hail, Queen of Heaven* came next. During the recital of the latter, I gazed up at Mum, who was singing in full soprano voice, dismayed and wondering how on earth she hit the high notes of 'the Ocean Star':

Nano never left the church without filling a small plastic Lourdes' bottle full of holy water from the font, to bless us all during the week, when we left our home, in the event of a thunder and lightning strike, or any other adversity.

Afterwards, the adults held their weekly meeting outside the surrounding walls of the church yard, discussing what did or didn't happen in the community that week, and their children, including Ted and me, made a dash to the nearby shop. A massive two-penny wafer ice cream was the choice for most.

When we arrived home, our pony got a big feed of oats, a bucket of water, and many long rubs along the length of her bare back from Grandpa. As Mum cooked a Sunday-morning treat for us all, our kitchen was filled with the appetising smell of sizzling sausages, bacon, and eggs. She served it with homemade bread and butter, and all plates were cleared in no time.

We made our Communion and Confirmation in this same Church. I recall Ted's First Holy Communion Day as if it were yesterday. Mum dressed him in a brown jacket, matching short pants, a white shirt and red tie. He wore brown brogue boots and knee-length socks. Pop had cut his hair the night before, and my big brother looked a million dollars. Thank Heavens Mum did not plonk a flat cap on his head.

A few days before Communion Day, Ted's First Confession went reasonably well, except for the fact that he told us that while he was telling his sins, an elderly priest with a weird looking combover hairstyle kept glaring back at him from the wooden confessional box.

During the many rehearsals for his First Holy Communion, his teacher instructed her class, "No matter what, my dear children, do not chew the host, but swallow it whole."

This instruction bothered Ted the most, and he told me so during the days leading up to his big event.

"Don't be worrying, Ted," I assured him, "all will be okay on your special day."

"I hope so, Maggie."

On his big day, when the priest gave him the host, he tried to swallow it as instructed, but it stuck to the roof of his mouth. He told Mum and me that he tried to dislodge it with his tongue, but it wouldn't budge. Not knowing what to do, he returned to his seat, knelt down, covered his face with his hands, and had a good chomp on the body of Christ.

Mum and Pop, helped by our grandparents, raised Ted, our sisters and me with the same faith that was handed down to them from previous generations. It was based on the fear of God, rather than the love of God. Thankfully, when I was growing up, the church's teaching had evolved, with more emphasis on love rather than fear, and this was much more in keeping with my nature, caring for animals and the environment.

School Days

Starting school as a young child can be challenging and overwhelming, and it was no different for me. There was only one consolation – my big brother Ted was always close by for support.

I spent my first day in school when I was five years old, and I have a vivid memory of Mum standing between the two white pillars of our farmyard gate with Sally our dog by her side. She stood there for what seemed like an eternity, waving her youngest child off to school as I walked off with Ted holding my hand. Her heart must have been breaking, as I know mine was. I had heard a multitude of stories from my older siblings about school, and to say the least, none of them would fill you with a glimmer of confidence in school life.

We wore regular clothes to school back then, as uniforms were unheard of in Gorse Valley. Mum washed each set of clothes on a Friday evening that our sisters, Ted, and I wore to school, and had them crispy dry in no time. Come Sunday evening, Nano made sure to iron and fold each garment and have them ready for us to wear to school for the next week. She used a black flat iron, made from solid metal, to remove the creases from our clothing. After heating it on a stand in front of the blazing open fire, she tested it to see if it was hot enough for use by sprinkling a little water on it.

During the long chilly days of winter, we wore brown leather brogue ankle boots, but as soon as May Day arrived and the roads shimmered with the heat of the sun, we walked to and from school barefoot, to save our boot leather for the coming winter. Stubbing a big toe off the loose stone chippings on the road was a regular occurrence during our sum-

36

mer trek to school in the morning and coming home in the evening. Then we had to navigate the hot bubbling tar patches, which could cause serious burns to the soles of our feet. Sometimes, it was necessary to walk on the soft grassy roadside edge to avoid such disasters. While the idea was to save the wear and tear of our boots, going barefoot to school was a time of joy for children, and everyone looked forward to the freedom of it.

Children then didn't have several pairs of footwear, having to make do with one pair of shoes for Sunday and other religious occasions and a pair of brogue boots for school. Having been made of pure leather, they had amazing lasting qualities and were handed down from one child to the next. In our family, they were passed down from Cait to Elizabeth and then to me.

After finishing our farm chores each morning, Ted and I left the cocoon of our home. Each with an army-green canvas satchel on our back, we grumbled and moaned, making every excuse why we shouldn't be going to school. We reckoned life would be much better, and far more beneficial to us, if we could stay at home helping on the farm. We whined so much that I am not sure the holy water Nano blessed us with each morning before we left could have done anything to allay our discontent.

The road to school was long and winding, framed for most of it by stone walls. On the left side, an enormous range of heathery mountains stretched high above for miles, while, on the right, an endless turquoise sea swelled in the distance below.

Stony rivers ran from the mountain top to the sea under some bridges along the road, and these were a huge source of distraction for Ted and me. We often stopped to watch the riffs and whirls of the running water, where birds searched for food and small fish swam on the riverbed. This wonder of nature took our minds off another unpleasant school day. On our way home, when our spirits were high, our voices bounced off the bridge roofs as we hollered underneath them.

An array of farmhouse buildings, with rusty corrugated iron sheds and some thatched cottages, were peppered along the length of the narrow road. A swathe of boggy or rush-filled fields, with furze bushes aplenty, separated the road from the mountains on one side and the sea on the other.

Our school of just three classrooms had large windows, and a front play yard enclosed by stone walls. Many shades of green fields surrounded it at the back, all peppered with bull-rushes. It was situated in the most idyllic setting between the mountains and sea, but these familiar features didn't make it any more pleasant for Ted and me.

Even though we were in two different class grades, we were lucky to be taught in the same classroom. In those days, each class had about six pupils, meaning a teacher taught two or more grade levels in the same space. Our desks were arranged in two rows, each containing children at various stages of education. My big brother and I were taught by Miss Hanan, who was tall, had short auburn hair, and wore spectacles and bright flowery dresses. The other six classes were taught by the headmaster, Mr Whitlock, and his wife. His skin looked like badly worn leather. He had a head full of white hair, a moustache, and he wore a brown tweed suit. His wife was much younger and had the appearance of a film star. She had soft shoulder-length black hair, wavy at the front and sides, and wore black body-hugging slimline dresses.

I could not imagine the conversations that went on between that pair when they arrived home each evening. I'm sure some of the children's ears were burning red during their discussions if they had a minor infraction in school.

It was the ethos of the school that most of our subjects were taught through the Irish language. This did not require much effort on our behalf, as Mum was a fluent speaker of the native tongue, with the result that speaking Irish came naturally to us. We had a textbook and writing copy for Irish, Maths, and English.

Ted and I were in the junior infant classes and our classroom was decorated from wall to wall with bright-coloured learning resources. Maths, alphabet, and rhyme charts decorated every available space on the four walls, and a large blackboard on an easel stood at the top of the room.

Miss Hanan wrote on the blackboard with *cailc* – chalk – and, when necessary, she wiped it off with a *glantoir* – a duster. It is well known by those who lived in that era, that teachers had the first drones – the blackboard *glantoir*, as many the time it flew across the classroom at an unsuspecting pupil who was misbehaving or not paying attention. I don't remember being one of its targets when I was daydreaming, but that was not beyond the realms of possibility back then. It was just the way things were. When pupils returned home and complained about the teacher to their parents, the complaints were not entertained.

We played with *mala* – plasticine – and empty rainbow-coloured thread spools to aid counting. *Mala* has many benefits, such as making little hands stronger and more dextrous to aid future writing.

Our school *mala* – elephant grey by a few weeks into the term – tested this theory beyond belief, as it was rock hard. We rolled it between the palms of our hands, and we rolled it again, then hand-kneaded it, even hammered it with our fists, but it didn't change its consistency. I'm not sure if our hands turned out to be more flexible but they did grow stronger.

When Miss Hanan bought new *mala* for us, we made stick men with it and used spent matchsticks for their neck, hands, and legs.

The clacking of those counting spools still echo in my head from back then, when the grumpy and impetuous Miss Hanan watched my paltry efforts to answer my given maths question. My anxiety over that particular school subject caused me to chew the top of my lead pencil, leaving bite marks all over it. I remember Grandpa paring that pencil with his tobacco penknife, as we didn't have pencil sharpeners at home or in school at that time.

Our lunch break was the most exciting part of our school day, and swapping lunches was always fun. One of my second cousins, a similar age to me, always had buttered bread and sugar sandwiches, and we often swapped for my soda-bread jam sandwiches.

After scoffing our lunches, we played games like chasing, ring-a-ring o'rosy, hide and seek, and skipping. Some boys played football, throwing their multi-coloured woollen jumpers on the pebbled yard to use as goal posts. Being a small school, with about fifty pupils at any one time, we were like one big family, jumping up and down, giggling and playing together. Not only were we all neighbouring children, quite a few of us were related.

Soon, Mr Whitlock appeared in the play yard, ringing his big solid brass handbell that had a dark-brown wooden handle, the loud clanging being a signal that lunchtime was finished, our fun was over, and we had to return to our classrooms, always with reluctance.

Obedience and respect for our teachers was of paramount importance. If we disobeyed the school rules, even in the slightest way, we got slaps, with a *bata* – a bamboo cane –

across the palms of our hands. We received the exact same punishment if we didn't know our Irish spellings or maths tables. Corporal punishment in school was rife back then.

Once, when the big boys of sixth class were playing in the yard, one boy, Maurice, threw one of the girl's shoes up on the school roof.

Mr Whitlock happened to be peering out the window of his classroom at that moment. He summoned all pupils of sixth class to his school room. Those of us who stood in a circle, laughing and watching the shoe spectacle in the yard, listened as quiet as mice outdoors, just under the open window, as the headmaster addressed the senior class.

"How did the shoe get up on the roof?" he asked.

"It fell up, Sir," answered one brave soul.

"That is ridiculous. I need an answer and I want it now. Who threw the shoe up on the roof?"

Complete silence filled the room. He asked the same question again.

"I ... I did, sir," Maurice answered, his voice quivering.

All of us gathered outside the window flinched on hearing the whacking of the *bata* landing three times at full force across Maurice's hand, and we slunk to the far end of the yard.

During winter, a turf fire was set in the open fireplace of each classroom by pupils from the most senior class; however, in wintry weather, those nearest the fire were the only ones to derive any heat from it.

The teachers stood beside the fireplace, with a full view of the pupils in front of them, sitting at big wooden writing desks. Two pupils sat at each desk and they had an inkwell each, full of blue ink. We had wooden dipping pens to write with, consisting of a simple wooden barrel with a basic metal nib on the end of it. It took great judgement and a steady hand to write with these implements. It was vital to pat the writing with blotting paper before turning the page over, as smudges or splashes of ink could destroy a written masterpiece.

Our bathroom facilities were, to say the least, lacking, as we didn't have toilets that flushed. Instead, a type of dry toilet was used, which had to be cleaned out every so often.

Two small sheds at the back of our school – or, to give them a fancier title, outhouses – with green doors, housed the toilets. We knew them as lavatories, and there was one for the boys and one for the girls. Minimal in design, each toilet was a large varnished wooden board with a gaping round hole in the centre, leading down to a cesspit.

The cesspit was washed clean on a regular basis with buckets of water from a nearby river. These were our meagre bathroom facilities, and the stench was such that little time was wasted within.

Ted had already been attending school for a little over a year and I had only been a pupil for a few weeks. I was happily playing in the school yard one day when I noticed my uncle just about to pass. Mum's brother, Uncle Bill, was on his way home from a local fair, a few towns away. His cart, drawn by his fawn donkey, was empty, with the exception of himself. My uncle's sandy-blonde hair was windblown and he was wearing his grey tweed working clothes.

"Uncle Bill, wait, wait for me, I'm coming with you," I shouted at the top of my voice, not understanding that I had some time left to spend in school that day.

He didn't stop, and I will never know if he heard me or not, but I cried buckets of tears when my uncle left me within the confines of school that day.

One particular morning while we were on our way to school, my big brother noticed that my head was downcast and sad.

"Why are you so sad, Maggie? Do you not want to go to school today?"

"Aw no, it's not about school, Ted, but I had a dream about Magic Maths last night."

"What is Magic Maths? I never heard of it before."

"Well, I dreamt that I could do Magic Maths, but the magic disappeared down behind the wardrobe. I searched and searched everywhere for it this morning, but I couldn't find it." I looked at him and shrugged. "I just wanted to find the Magic Maths, Ted, as the maths in school is very hard."

"Don't be worrying about your maths in school today, Maggie. We will search when we get home this evening and see if we can find your Magic Maths."

The big clock on the front wall of our classroom seemed to malfunction, as most days it ticked ever so slowly. But when its hands, at last, read three o'clock, you couldn't see us for dust. Ted and I, along with all the other pupils, were out that green school gate as quick as our legs could carry us.

A sad and lingering memory about our journey from school will be with me forever. On our way home each evening, a spiky blonde-haired boy, with bright slanted blue eyes and smartly dressed, played in the yard of his parents' farm. He was about eight years old and he seemed to want to join in our fun.

We always stopped to chat with him, but no matter how hard we tried, he failed to verbally respond. It appeared that he spent his days in that farmyard and never got to venture outside. The two of us were heartbroken for him and wished that he would someday take part in our homebound fun.

One day, when we got home from school, we told Mum about him. She put her arms around us and said, "Ah, Ted and Maggie, that is Ben, the little Down Syndrome boy. Don't be worrying about him, he is happy with his life." She didn't say 'Down Syndrome' of course, there was another word for it then, but she was a kind woman, my mum, and would never use a word to give offence, if there was another to use.

While we didn't understand her explanation, we continued to stop and pay him attention on our homeward journey from school.

But, on another occasion, I asked Mum, "Why can't Ben go to school with Ted and me?"

"It's okay, Maggie, don't be anxious about Ben. I know his mum well and she teaches him little by little."

It was many years later when I realised that Ben needed special education and it was not available in schools in Ireland in the 1950s.

Other days, on our way home from school, my brother and I, and other children, would hightail it inside a stone-wall ditch at the sight of a tattily dressed scary woman coming towards us, putting fear in our hearts. We would peep over the wall to check if she'd passed, and only then continue on our journey home. Our fear of this woman originated from stories we heard within our community, and Heaven only knows why or what the purpose of it was.

One day, the two of us were walking home from school, and we must have got distracted and dropped our guard. Before we could react, the scary woman appeared out of nowhere and stood straight as a poker in front of us.

"Hello, Ted and Maggie."

Surprised that she even knew our names, I grabbed Ted's arm and neither of us could utter a sound, trembling, and terrified of what she'd do to us. She asked us what class we were in, and she also continued with some other small talk. To our astonishment, she took some wrapped blackjack sweets out of her bag and gave them to us. We were amazed. The scary woman could not have been more pleasant. From that day forward, we chatted with her on a regular basis, as did our neighbouring friends after we told them our delightful tale.

Each school day, our little dog Sally waited for us at our farmyard gate, wagging her tail at a furious rate as she welcomed us home, and she filled our hearts with joy. We knew it had to be tough for her not having us there during the day, though I was sure she kept busy doing her jobs around the farm.

School days can conjure a powerful mixture of emotions, good and bad, and it is often said that school days are the best days of your life, but for Ted and me, staying at home and doing farm chores was far better than attending school.

A Motorcar

Pop had accomplished his dream from our stay in London and he built himself a carpentry workshop, as building work was another one of his skills. With his ultimate brand carpentry tools, he made kitchen furniture, toys, and much more from the finest wood. Red spoked donkey cartwheels, and blue and burgundy latticed hemp-rope chairs were his most sought-after pieces.

After some time had passed and with his carpentry venture in Gorse Valley, as well as some income from our farm, he accumulated some savings. His next step up in life was to buy a car. Having grown used to driving from place to place in London, he felt it was necessary to have a car in Ireland. This enabled our family to have freedom and independence. At this time in Gorse Valley, it was rare for anyone to have a motorcar, as they were too expensive to buy. Our normal mode of transport and that of everyone else was either a donkey and cart or a pony and trap.

Pop grinned from ear to ear when it arrived outside our back door. A gleaming black Ford Prefect, and I can still remember its number plate: ZX811. His face lit up like the sun when neighbouring men gathered around his spotless vehicle. Not having seen many cars close up, they admired its curves, lustrous chrome, and bright red taillights. They raised the bonnet and peeped into its engine bay, and when Pop cranked the engine, all clapped with wonderment and delight.

My brother and I were fascinated by the switches and instruments on the gleaming dashboard. At every opportunity, and when his back was turned, we would hop into the car and fiddle with anything we could put our hands on. Just above the steering wheel were two clocks. One was a speedometer and mileage recorder, the other contained a fuel gauge and warning lights, but what interested us most were the ignition switch and the choke. We knew these were instrumental in the car starting up. I remember Pop having to pull out the choke on the dashboard and adjust it before the car would start.

Pop managed to find a new excuse every morning to put off his work. He would wake up before us all and get the important things out of the way before breakfast, like the milking, mucking out the sheds, and feeding the animals. Afterwards, he would sit at the table with us and ponder aloud, "I think the bran for the cows is running low, we'd better go into town for some more."

And off we would go, rattling away down the narrow winding roads, six of us crammed into the back and Grandpa and Pop in front. No matter our destination, Pop always managed to find a way to drive through big towns, slowing the car and hooting the horn until the residents went to their windows and saw him passing. Then he'd speed off, leaving an impressive dust cloud behind him.

On one occasion, when we were going for a Sunday drive with our uncle Peter and our three cousins who came to visit from London, which they often did, our uncle decided he would drive our automobile. To Ted's annoyance, I kicked up an unholy ruckus because I only trusted Pop, with his Ferrari driving skills, to drive our car.

"Maggie, Uncle Peter is a good driver, you know," Ted exclaimed.

"No, no, Ted, I want Pop to drive our car."

Ted tried to shush me, as he didn't want Uncle Peter to hear what my outburst was about, but I continued my discord under my breath.

On our Sunday drive, it was necessary for us to go around the most dangerous bends in the county. The horseshoe and hairpin bends were not for the fainthearted. As we rounded them, the two of us, and our cousins – two boys and a girl – were catapulted from one side of the car to the other and back again. There were no seat belts in those days, and humpback bridges in the middle of these dangerous bends did nothing to ease our anxiety. Our hearts were in our mouths. Thankfully, Pop was driving our car at this time.

On another occasion, Ted, our sisters and I were walking to school with our army-green canvas satchels on our backs. When we reached the next townland, Timothy, a friend of Pop's, was scratching his head as he peered under the bonnet of his car. He hadn't the slightest knowledge about mechanical matters.

"Come here for a minute, Maggie," he said, on noticing that my older siblings were otherwise occupied, "I cannot start my car."

As luck would have it, his car was similar to our motorcar. After having a quick look at his predicament, I drew his attention to the choke switch on the dashboard.

"Timothy, you need to pull out the choke switch for your car to start."

He adjusted the choke, gave the crank handle a few turns, and, like magic, his engine hummed back into life.

Timothy had no bother starting his car from that day onwards. For years afterwards, he told the story to many people, about how a six-year-old little girl was able to instruct him on how to start his car.

I vividly remember one summer, when our UK cousins were visiting us yet again, and one of the boys – Pete, named after his father – had two beautiful and treasured toy cars, which he rarely left out of his sight. He stored them in a shoe box, which he called their garage. Gleaming old-style cars, one was black similar to Pop's Prefect and the other one was two-tone grey.

I longed to play with them, and when he was distracted one day, I snuck into the parlour room, where I knew he had hidden his much-loved toys. For what seemed like an hour or more, I was overjoyed playing with them, pushing them forwards and backwards along the floor.

The parlour door creaked open and Pete burst in. He grabbed his treasured toys out of my hands, saying in his cockney accent, "Maggie, they are my cars. How dare you play wif 'em."

I let out a scream, annoyed that my play opportunity had been discovered.

Mum ran from the kitchen to separate the two of us. "Stop fighting. You can take turns at playing with the toys." Which we did, but reluctantly so.

After some time, Pop built a lean-to shed for his car. It was open plan, with four wooden poles and rafters holding up a corrugated iron roof. He'd wash and shine his car on a regular basis and do any maintenance work it needed in the shelter of this building.

If you have risen a few steps up in the world by further education and blood, sweat, and a few tears, like Pop did, you're entitled to flaunt it. He was like a member of royalty, driving his shiny car here, there, and everywhere, and I was mighty proud of it too.

Shopping Back Then

Our local grocery shop was a seven-minute walk away. It was here Mum bought any extra weekly messages we needed: flour to make homemade bread; sugar; tea; salt; and much more. She brought home these necessities in what we called a message bag – a large reusable cotton tote bag.

Sometimes a barter system was used: Mum 'sold' the free-range eggs our wonderful hens produced to the shopkeeper Bob, and he gave her groceries in exchange for their worth. Both of their faces were radiant at these times, indicating that bartering in this way suited them to perfection. Afterwards, the shopkeeper sold the fresh eggs to someone else who didn't have laying hens at home.

A white vintage-looking mechanical weighing scales took pride of place on the counter. This one had a large red dial arrow at the front – similar to that of a clock – and it measured in pounds and ounces. Everything was weighed loose – there was no pre-packaging then, Sugar, for instance, was ladled from an enormous sack into a stainless-steel bowl and placed on springs at the front of the scales. Small round steel weights, of various values, were placed on a sprung plate at the back of it, depending on what was being weighed. For sugar, it would be the big pound weight, for sweets, just an ounce or, if we were being treated, a quarter (four ounces). The dial arrow indicated when an equilibrium was reached between back and front – for a big, clumsy-looking old thing, it was surprisingly accurate.

A cash register stood beside the weighing scales – an old gold-coloured mechanical model. It had a small number-display window on the front but didn't output receipts.

When Bob wanted to work out how much a particular list of groceries cost, he typed in each amount mechanically, clunkily so, similar to that of an old typewriter. When he had inputted all figures, a drawer on the till opened with a cha-ching bell sound. It left Bob scratching his head, as it was a mere adding machine, leaving him to figure out how much change he needed to give his customer.

All of the children in our neighbourhood, including Ted and me, would regularly run to this shop and spend our pennies buying sumptuous wafer ice creams, Peggy's Legs, Sweet Cigarettes, Black Jacks, and Bull's Eye sweets. When I got pennies for sweets in those days, happiness swelled within me.

The shop, a room in Bob's house, had a counter made of mahogany, with glass-panelled displays underneath. It stretched around the length and breadth of the shop in an 'L' shape. All sorts of brightly coloured sweet jars, bars of chocolate, penny bars, and much more were stored in it, while newspapers were stacked on the counter itself. On the many wooden shelves that reached the ceiling behind where Bob stood, an array of groceries was displayed: Rinso; Lifebuoy carbolic soap; cigarettes; tobacco; alcohol; and the list goes on.

I remember well a visit to Bob's shop when I was a child. It was summertime, and I was dressed in my Sunday-best clothing: a gingham cotton dress, matching blue hand-knitted cardigan, sparkling white ankle socks, and shiny patient shoes. And, as always, Mum had plonked a large bow on top of my head, but it fell off as my hair was so silky. I ran to the shop at lightning speed; the two treasured copper pennies I clutched – 1d pingins, with a hen and chicks depicted on them – made my hand hot and moist. The counter was too high for me, and I had to stand on my tippy toes while peering up asking Bob for sweets. When he had them ready in a small brown paper bag, he leaned over the counter and handed them down to me. I, in turn, reached up and handed him my two hot pennies.

Ted accompanied me to the shop that day, as he always did, and bought sweets, too, but unlike me he wasn't short in stature and had no difficulty asking for his stash of goodies from our friendly shopkeeper. We said goodbye to Bob and ambled home delightfully munching our multicoloured confectionary.

Customers could also buy groceries from Bob on tick – a pay-later arrangement. He would record the grocery purchase of each family in a 'little red book' assigned to them, which he safely kept on a shelf in the shop. When they sold a calf, a pig, or when their cheque arrived from the creamery cooperative, they wasted no time in paying him their debt and he duly ticked it off as paid.

Goods were carefully and organically packaged in the shop, as they were in most rural towns in those days, in brown paper bags. Sometimes the bags were tied with string, depending on the size of goods bought, and handed to the buyer by the shopkeeper with a broad smile.

The shop was also our post office, and they sold paraffin oil and some animal feedstuff too. It was here the locals made telephone calls, as not a single other person in Gorse Valley possessed a house phone back then. They also received telegrams there, which were dreaded, as they mostly contained sad news, like a loved one having passed on. The sender, usually a relative living elsewhere, but mostly abroad, would write a short message on a telegraph blank, similar to a writing notepad, paying for each word written. The message was transcribed into morse code and transmitted over telegraph lines to the shop. Bob then notified the receiver of the message that a telegram awaited him or her, and it was a regular occurrence to see them leave the shop with downcast heads and choked with tears.

Thank goodness they didn't store teak or mahogany coffins in the shop, as they did in similar establishments throughout rural Ireland. I had a severe aversion to coffins or anything related to them, as I do to this day.

Bob's shop was an important part of the social fabric of Gorse Valley, as members of the community would go there to gather local news, have a laugh and chat with neighbours, as well as buying whatever commodities they needed.

Clothes shopping online or in a mall was unheard of in Gorse Valley, and we didn't have wardrobes full of trendy clothes. We had a brown teak wardrobe upstairs, in a nook at the end of the landing, which contained our Sunday-best clothing – one precious outfit for each family member. For occasions such as First Communions and Confirmations, our clothes were bought in a shop during a rare visit to a big town. With pride, Mum made sure we were immaculately dressed for Sunday Mass or for these events.

Mum took being immaculately dressed to a new level. When washing our cotton garments, she used 'Reckitt's Bag of Blue' – a blue-coloured rinse – and when the clothes were steeped in it, they became snow white. Also, our bed sheets got a similar but more rigorous treatment. She boiled them in a big pot over the fire, having added the same household product. I distinctly remember how she lifted the sparkling white but boiling-hot sheets out of the pot with wooden tongs. She wrung the heavy sodden bedclothes with her bare hands and hung them on the clothesline in the haggard, where they and our other garments were crisply dried by the four winds. I remember her regularly saying, "There is nothing nicer than seeing a long line of clothes blowing and drying on a lively windy day."

Our ironing queen Nano used 'Robin Starch' on shirts, especially on the collars to stiffen them – a handy trick she learned while working in the Big Houses of the gentry. It was a stiff white powder, similar to cornflour, and water was added to it. Nano immersed the Sunday-best removable shirt collars in it and then ironed them with her flat black iron – a box iron. Grandpa and Pop took immense pride in wearing their highly starched stiff collar shirts to church or funerals.

Otherwise, Mum handmade all of our school outfits, our dresses, Ted's trousers, and our old duds – our farming clothes. She was a dab hand at using a foot-operated Singer sewing machine, and patterns for sizing purposes. Sometimes, she handknitted jumpers and cardigans with new wool. Other times, she would rip asunder an adult garment that had some wear left in parts of it and knitted smaller garments for us from it. She also sewed skirts for us girls and short pants for Ted from pieces of fabric she bought by the skin of her teeth from a drapery shop. Clothes were handed down from Cait to Elizabeth, and then to me. Socks were darned and clothes were patched, with nothing ever going to waste.

One of her tougher tasks was making bedsheets and pillowcases from white cotton Odlum's flour sacks, and I remember that huge orange logo of the owl's head on the sack. Mum painstakingly ripped all of the thread that bound the bags together and, when opened out flat, it took four to make a double sheet and one to make a pillowcase. She scrubbed and scrubbed that owl logo off each sack, then washed them several times to remove any trace of the orange print. After sewing the pieces together on her sewing machine, they made long-lasting bedsheets and pillowcases.

Simplicity was the essence of life in Gorse Valley. Whatever happened on our farm holding was a carbon copy of what took place on neighbouring farmsteads. Everyone had similar food and clothing, and there was no keeping up with or trying to be better than each other.

Mountainside Adventure

The early morning mist covering the mountains had already cleared, and the rising sun cast a rosy hue across the sky. For Ted and me, the mountainside above our farm enticed us to explore this vast expanse of mysterious roughhewn terrain.

After a hurried breakfast, Ted donned a T-shirt, short pants, and wellington boots. As a girl rooted in farming life, I dressed similarly, and we began our mountainside adventure. We entered the flora and fauna-laden narrow boreen bordering our farmyard and travelled a good distance upwards to the mountain.

"Let's go faster, Maggie," Ted called, striding ahead of me, "it's taking us too long to get to the hillside."

"Okay, okay," I replied, gasping and battling for air," "I'm going as fast as I can."

He turned around, grabbed my hand, and together we ran to the mountainside at a much quicker pace.

Having left the boreen behind, we were amongst the wide expanse of purple heather, about halfway up the hill. Our eyes bulged on noticing some green, grassy, uneven bumps and hollows strewn with rocks. Buried deep amongst the heather, they stretched in a winding line from the mountain top and downwards to the sea. On further inspection, we realised it was a concrete water pipeline.

We were able to gain access to this monstrous construction of water pipes through child-size openings at two separate places. When we peeped in, it became obvious that the pipeline was bone dry. Like true adventurers, we crawled through them, from one end to the other and back again, umpteen times.

Having the need to rest, we sat for a while on the highland and pondered the beauty of our surroundings. It was so quiet, as if the world stood still, with the aroma of the purple heather filling the air.

Far off in the distance, we noticed fishing boats sailing the briny waters. A few men were pulling the oars, and some were casting nets to catch shoals of fish for market day. We could just about make out other fishermen standing on the strand, mending their fishing nets or tarring their upturned boats.

"I would love to go fishing on those boats with the fishermen one day," Ted said.

"You will, Ted. I know you will someday."

We resumed our pipeline scurrying, giggling with delight, our screams bouncing and echoing off the walls of the hollow pipes. One time, Ted bumped his head off the upper side of the pipe but there was no stopping him. Our knees were red and skinned from crouching and creeping along the concrete surface but, unperturbed, we continued scurrying back and forth through the tight tunnels.

Without warning, an enormous gush of water torrented through the pipeline from above. Luckily, at this moment, we were at the bottom opening and, on hearing the rush of water heading towards us, we jumped to safety. Ted jumped first and grabbed my hand, helping me to escape the surge, and just in time.

Mounds of clay had gathered further up the mountain and blocked the water from passing through the pipeline. However, the sheer force of the water must have worn it down over time. My big brother and I were blissfully unaware that we could have been swept at high speed, down through the pipes to the sea.

Having lost track of time, we knew Mum would be wondering where we had disappeared to, so we needed to get home as soon as possible. We scampered through the thick undergrowth of the hillside and down the boreen at lightning speed, stopping halfway down at a well for a drink of water, which we scooped into our mouths with cupped hands.

We set off again, fast, but then Ted hollered in pain, holding his leg and limping. He sat down and I rubbed his calf muscle as he groaned. After a few minutes, the worst of the pain subsided and we continued our journey but at a slower pace, as Ted didn't want his leg to cramp again.

A little way on, our dog Sally came around the corner of the boreen, panting with her tongue hanging out. The white blaze of hair down her front was grubby, as she must have run through mud. Our sweet Sally had sensed our commotion from a long distance away and hurried to our rescue.

When we arrived home, Mum was pacing back and forth, worried out of her mind, thinking something bad had happened to us. After taking a few minutes to calm down, she listened as we recalled our adventure up the mountainside and about our exploration of the concrete water pipeline. But we didn't tell her about our narrow escape, of nearly being swept down to the sea by the torrent of water.

We were normally free to roam the area of our townland without any restrictions, as it posed little or no danger, but, on this occasion, Mum was adamant that we should never explore those pipelines again. Even though we didn't tell her about our near disaster, she was, of course, aware of the potential danger up the mountain.

"Where on earth were Ted and Maggie," Pop asked, having not laid eyes on us all morning.

As ever, Mum's thoughtfulness and protection of her children was at the ready. "They were across the road helping Mrs O'Brien, fetching water from the well and turf for her fire."

"Well, to heck with Mrs O'Brien," grumpy old Pop said, with steam coming out of his ears, "they should have been here. I had work for them to do."

This was a lie on Mum's behalf, knowing we hadn't been across the road helping Mrs O'Brien. She knew that, sometimes, a harmless fib could prevent a less than favourable outcome. Before all hell broke loose, and Pop had a conniption, we did his requested farm chores, mucking out the calf shed and pigsty. Ted did the chores without complaint, but I did shoddy work in protest at Pop's outburst.

Pop's one mission appeared to be to make life hard for us children. If we were attempting to do a new farm chore, he never explained the proper way of doing it but let us fall into the trap of doing the task incorrectly. Red in the face, he would then explain to us how the job should be done. Maybe he was trying to toughen us up, or maybe he lacked empathy for children. His intent was hard to fathom. We preferred to do farm chores working alongside Grandpa, but there were many times we reluctantly had to help our father.

I remember one particular day as if it were yesterday, as my heart was breaking for poor Ted. Pop was cutting wood for the fire in the haggard with a heavy-duty crosscut saw, and he asked Ted to help him.

The saw was a huge, heavy and long cutting implement, with a wooden handle on each side. Ted tried to do his best, even though this task was more suitable for two grown men. Even being a big burly lad, he didn't have the strength to hold this monstrous gadget upright while Pop swished it back and forth through the wood. Tears streamed down Ted's cheeks and Pop was red faced with anger.

Luckily, Grandpa came along and intervened. He didn't just help Pop, he reprimanded him for the hardship he was putting Ted through. I put my arms around Ted, gave my father a killer sideways' glance, and we ran indoors to Mum.

Later that night, while we were dozing off to sleep, Mum told us our bedtime story and said our nighttime prayers with us. Before she left our room, we barely heard her say, "Ted and Maggie, have a good night's sleep and don't pay any heed to your father. Some days, he is a cantankerous old coot."

"Night, night, Mum, we won't," we mumbled in unison.

Unlike Pop, Mum had an amazing sense of humour. Sometimes, she would even laugh at his angry outbursts when something trivial happened. Maybe Cait or Elizabeth forgot to do their homework, or Grandpa forgot to close a gate. Trivial matters that were easily rectified irked him, but Mum could see the futility of his anger.

The next morning, as we awoke from our slumbers, we reminisced about our mountainside adventure. While we were now aware of the dangers of the water pipeline, we were sure the mountain terrain held many more mysteries. We promised each other we would visit it again someday, and maybe we would find the stone-built dugout shelter Grandpa had told us about many times.

Hospital Stay

When I was a little more than six years old, it was necessary for me to spend some time in hospital, as I had to have my glands removed. At least that's what I was told. But many years afterwards, and on investigation, I discovered those glands were my tonsils.

One would think I travelled to the hospital in Pop's Ford Prefect, or maybe a kind relation took me in the comfort of a nice motorcar, accompanied by my mum. Not at all. On a dull and cold November morning, Pop was taking two pigs to the fair, which was several townlands away from our home. He borrowed a dusty pickup truck from a neighbour for the journey. I was dressed in a warm red coat and hat, and Mum sat me up on the long bench seat beside Pop.

"We have to go now, Kate," he said, "as I need to be at the fair early, to have the best chance of selling these pigs."

Tears welled in Mum's eyes as she waved me goodbye. Poor Ted's face was downcast too. The pigs were squealing a little in the back of the pickup, but after some time they quietened down, with the motion of the truck lulling them to sleep.

We arrived at the enormous, ancient red brick building, where an ambulance in the courtyard filled me with trepidation. When we climbed the big stone steps leading to a dark mahogany double door, I looked inside, my gaze swivelling over the busy waiting room. Uniformed doctors and nurses passed by, busily going hither and thither, opening and closing doors, with the nauseous aroma of hospital antiseptic wafting through the air.

Pop had a few quiet words with a lady dressed in a blue and white uniform. He left me in her care and rushed off to sell his pigs. Along came a nun, one of the charitable order of sisters who managed the care of patients at the hospital. She was dressed in a flowing black gown, wearing a matching veil with a white band across the front and large brown wooden rosary beads dangling from her neck. She was quite scary looking to a little girl and she glared at me down her nose, her nostrils flaring; it made her look angry, though for all I knew, I suppose, she could have just been really busy.

"Come with me now, young lady," she said.

She swirled around and barged forwards, her head in the air and her black tunic fluttering behind her. Apprehensive, I followed her, holding a little bag in my hand that Mum gave me. Chills crept into my spine as we walked from one long dark corridor to the next, passing many small rooms with glass panels at the top of each one.

The black-clad apparition left me high and dry in one such room. Before leaving, she commanded me to change into my pyjamas and get into a steel-framed bed, with dark green linen matching that of the dim hallway.

With butterflies in my stomach, I grabbed the cold metal bedrail and pulled myself onto the mattress. I was all alone, with the exception of an old box radio on low, playing music in the corner. Someone coughed in the next room, the sound harsh and hacking. My tears flowed like a river, as I missed Mum, Ted, and my family.

Later that day, I heard a commotion coming from outside the building. I jumped out of bed, peered out of the window and saw children playing on slides and swings in a nearby park. Even though it appeared to be a cold windswept day, I wished with all my heart that I could join in their laughter and fun. But that was not to be, as I was instructed to get into that bed by the nun.

As the dark evening approached, I was ravishing hungry, but I could not eat any food, required to fast because of having my procedure early the next morning. Petrified that the bossy nun would return, I hugged my pillow and fell asleep. I dreamt that Pop collected me when he was finished at the fair but, on waking, it broke my heart to realise I was still in the same room.

My tonsils were removed that morning and thank Heavens I have no recollection of that event. Sometime later, the flared-nostril nun offered me ice cream to eat. I remember devouring it – the best-tasting dessert ever.

The next day, the same individual served me stewed apple and custard dessert, but the stewed apple was lumpy and I refused to eat it. She enticed and coaxed me, but her pleading was in vain. Even when she got annoyed with me, I still wouldn't put a taste of it inside my lips.

"I want my mum. I want her now," I blubbered right into her face,

She glared at me. "Your mum will be here tomorrow."

During a routine check the next day, the same dark figure stuck a long glass tube with a silver piece at the end under my tongue and wrapped a pressurised band around my arm. As far as I can remember, I ate regular meals that day. She stomped across the room several times and did nothing to allay my loneliness for my mum. But, despite her snappy answer the day before, no trace of Mum arrived that day. She didn't drive and I somehow understood, even as a small child, that it would be difficult for her to visit me.

Bright and early the next morning, Grandpa appeared at the door of the room I was confined in. I ran to him and jumped into his arms, hugging and kissing him.

"Come on, get dressed, Maggie, I am taking you home today."

"Okay, Grandpa." And I wasted no time changing into regular clothes.

Before we left the confines of the hospital, my lofty carer complained to Grandpa that I would not eat the beautiful dessert she had given me two days previously. He ignored her remarks and we continued on our way.

Once we reached the hospital courtyard, Grandpa put me on the carrier of his big black bike. He threw his leg over the saddle and began pedalling, and it wasn't long before it picked up speed. As we rattled our way along the rough, bumpy road, I gazed around at the wonders of nature surrounding us: the rush-filled fields, the mountains, and the sea. We giggled as we sped around each bend along our journey.

When we eventually arrived home, Grandpa took me off his bike, and I burst in the back door to see Mum standing in the middle of the kitchen with her hands on her hips and a huge smile beaming across her face.

Ted put his arms around me and said, "I missed you, Maggie, and I am so, so glad you are home."

"Oh, I missed you too, Ted."

Nano hugged me. "Thank Heavens you are home, girleen."

During my teenage years, I was taught in second-level school by an amazing order of nuns. They cared for each child in the school as if they were their own. But, as far as I was concerned, the dark-clad scary nun I encountered during my hospital stay when my tonsils were being removed did not live up to this standard of care. Later that evening, I candidly told Mum that I never ever wanted to go back to that dank red brick building where she lived.

Mum

God made my mum,
with gentle, helping hands,
And a caring spirit,
that always understands.

He took the brightest stars,
and put them in her eyes.
He made her good and kind,
wonderful and wise.

God made my mum,
as perfect as can be.
He filled her heart with love,
that overflowed for me.

– Unknown –

Danjoe and Ada

Our neighbour, Danjoe, lived just to the west of our farm. A warm-hearted and red-faced stocky man in his early fifties, he wore brown corduroy trousers and a brown jumper, and forever wore a flat cap turned sideways on his head, a bit like Pop. It provided cover for his balding polished dome. Whether he was working on his farm or attending Sunday church services, a change of clothing was deemed unnecessary.

He and Ada, his wife, had ten children who ranged in age from eight to twenty, two of whom were living in London. Having a big family there was always an abundance of fun and laughter in their two-storey house.

My brother and I had the pleasure of having breakfast with Danjoe on the odd occasion. After finishing his breakfast, and still sitting by the kitchen table, he donned his army-green wellington boots. He did not fit them on any old way. Instead, he pulled them right up his legs to his knees, then folded down the top four inches of each boot so they did not restrict his movement. With the inside cream lining of his boots turned outwards, he was ready to tackle his daily farm chores.

He tended to his zoo of farm animals each day, sometimes with beads of perspiration upon his brow. While he loved all of his animals dearly, he paid particular attention to his plough horse, Molly. A chestnut-brown gentle giant with four white fetlocks, she was his pride and joy. Whether she needed daily exercise or not, he put on her halter and paraded her up and down the roadway in front of their house.

Ada had a thick mop of black hair, in complete contrast to her pallid-white skin. I remember her dressed in a black and white flowery apron over a black dress, and she was the same vintage as her husband. Her favourite part of life was being a home maker, rearing their children, along with a gaggle or two of geese.

The fun in their home reached its peak when their two eldest sons arrived home on holiday from London. Danjoe played music on his old black and white Horner button accordion, and dancing was an every-night occurrence. Neighbours young and old joined in to celebrate their homecoming, including Ted and me. The boys' hair was groomed in Teddy Boy quiff style, and they wore 'Edwardian' drape jackets, with shiny, pointy-toe shoes.

We often found small empty shampoo and toothpaste sachets scattered in their front yard after their return from London. We sniffed each one and I loved the musky smell of the shampoo sachets.

"Maggie, what are those sachets for?" Ted asked.

"Oh, they are for washing your hair and teeth."

They fascinated us, as we had never laid eyes on such personal hygiene products before. Our hair was washed with Lifebuoy soap and we never even heard of toothpaste. To clean our teeth at any time of day was unheard of.

To all and sundry, it would appear that this couple had an ideal family life. But, many years later, and even though I thought the world of Danjoe, Mum enlightened me that he caused his wife much trouble and many a sleepless night. Ada had a harsh dislike of times when her husband visited the local public house. A creamy pint of black porter was his absolute favourite beverage. Unfortunately, he had a habit of remaining in that particular establishment for far too long.

On each occasion, before he left the house, worried that one alcoholic beverage too many could impair his judgement cycling home, Ada would inevitably ask, "How long will you be, Danjoe?"

"Ach, don't be worrying, Ada, I will only be a half an hour or so."

To her absolute disgust, three hours later, he would stagger in the back door. Not alone was his staggering the issue, Ada was aware that his journey home had to be navigated while he was under the influence of too much alcohol. A mile-long journey, wobbling from one side of the road to the other on his old rattling bike, was unthinkable.

One dark winter's evening, Ada was finding it hard to close her eyes. Startled by a loud bang on the back door, she jumped out of her warm bed and scurried down the stairs. On opening the door, her face burned red at the sight of her drunken husband standing there in the company of another man, six-foot tall and clad in an official Garda uniform. After finding her intoxicated husband on the side of the road, with grazed hands and a grubby face, the local officer thought it best to accompany him home.

With a deep frown, Garda Seán explained that their journey home had not been an easy one. Somewhere along the way, and in the dark of night, Danjoe hit the road with a crash. The on-duty Garda went to great lengths assuring Ada that he had succeeded, with the exception of a few hair-raising moments, to bring her husband safely home.

After staggering in, umpteen apologies came from the bold Danjoe, many of them with slurred speech.

"So, so sorry, Ada. I won't stay as long the next time, believe me, I won't stay as long the next time."

Mortified by the official Garda visit and his encounter with the law, Ada was beside herself with rage. With enormous disgust in her voice, she exclaimed, "That's it, me boyo, enough is enough. There will not be a next time. Over my dead body will you ever make another visit to that hell hole."

Come the next morning, it was left to Ada and their children to do all the farm chores, including milking the cows. Meanwhile, her husband was unable to raise his hungover head from his pillow, though after a few loud shouts and yells from the farmyard, he dragged himself out of the bed. With his head hanging low, he brought the milk churns to the creamery onboard the cart, pulled by his little donkey.

On the way back home, and still rather flushed in the face, he did not forget our mutual neighbour, Mrs O'Brien. He called by the local store and bought her usual daily newspaper and groceries.

"Would you like a cup of tea, Danjoe?" she asked when he arrived at her house.

"Ach, sure, I'll have a small sup in the bottom of a cup."

His response had nothing to do with him being hungover – it was just his polite way of saying he would like some tea. However, the cup of tea did somewhat clear his head and, leaving Mrs O'Brien with her daily shopping, he returned home.

There, he found Ada sitting at the table, bowed low, holding her head between her hands. Knowing he had created untold anguish for his wife, he cried, "As true as God is my judge, Ada, I will never again put a drop of the black stuff inside my lips."

With trepidation, Ada accepted his promise, and they continued their daily chores.

Not long afterwards, he was chatting with Jockser, a friend from a nearby town, and he confided in him about his alcoholic tendencies, and how they were destroying his life.

"Well now, my dear man, I will tell you a tale that will end your troubles. Old William from over the hills had similar problems to yours, but they ended abruptly."

"How did that happen?" Danjoe asked.

"William had severe pains in his stomach for many years," Jockser replied, "and one day, they were absolutely excruciating, and he ended up in hospital. After thorough examination, his doctors realised he was in liver failure because of alcohol poisoning. They did their utmost, trying all sorts of medication to try and save his life but, three days later, William passed on to his eternal reward."

Danjoe had made a promise of sobriety to Ada, and his chat with Jockser reinforced it. He never let a drop of the black stuff pass his lips from then onwards.

Mrs O'Brien

Mrs O'Brien lived across the road from our farm in a wee cottage, nestled by tall trees. Her quaint cottage was the only home in our neighbourhood which was not part of a farm holding.

She was a heavily built, white-haired woman, always clad in a widow's black dress, and wore a scarf on her head patterned with a plethora of bright-pink flowers. Her hearing in one ear wasn't great. If she really wanted to hear a particular conversation, she tugged at her scarf and pulled it behind the troublesome ear. Failing that, and if she still couldn't hear what was being said, she would interrupt with, "Will you stop whisperin', for Pete's sake, I can't hear you."

As a result of a traumatic experience while living in the USA, she never moved from the surroundings of her new home in Gorse Valley. Her only supports were us, her nearest neighbours, and Danjoe.

In broad daylight, two hooded burglars had smashed a rear window and broke into her USA home. They ordered her into a linen closet at gunpoint, then ransacked her much-loved home and stole her TV and items of jewellery, including some of sentimental value. One was her wedding ring, received from her late husband when they were wed fifty-five years earlier. O'Brien was her marriage name, as her husband was originally from Ireland.

She emerged from the closet, terrified, and took great care as she peeped around the rooms of her home to make sure the burglars were gone. Still shocked, she lifted the phone and alerted her neighbour, who dashed over to help her.

He contacted the police and helped her to clean up the appalling mess. The contents of drawers, cupboards, and her closets were strewn across the floor in every room. They broke ornaments, upturned furniture, and shattered the glass of cupboards in her kitchen.

A good friend came to stay with her for a while because she was scared to live on her own after the burglary. It wasn't long before that they realised she couldn't stay there, so they planned the sale of her home and her move to Ireland.

A short while after she arrived in Gorse Valley, Danjoe presented her with a black and white terrier dog, as a welcome gift, and for company. She named him Toby. Along with her little dog, she soon settled in her new home, and felt safe in our rural community, between the mountains and sea.

The whitewashed walls of her burnished-gold thatched cottage gleamed like snow, and its glossy red door glistened in the sun. An array of potted plants was artfully arranged around the door, and an ornamental black cat sat on the windowsill, right next to it.

Before Mrs O'Brien came to live amongst us, the cottage had been given a complete makeover. I clearly recall its thatched roof had gone into disrepair and decay – it was leaking and a multitude of different bird species had made their nests on it.

A professional thatching team from another townland came daily for about two weeks and rethatched it. With wooden ladders, they climbed up on the roof and painstakingly removed some of the old rotten thatch, then covered the entire roof with well-seasoned straw, which was held in place with hazel rods or scallops. When they were finished their work, the roof looked like a work of art, with a beautifully defined ridge and a golden-straw covering. I remember Grandpa remarking, "That is powerful work. Well, done, men," a compliment they thanked him for.

My brother and I fetched water from the well and brought in a basket of turf for her almost daily.

I would often remind Ted, "Let's go, we need to help Mrs O'Brien."

"Sure, Maggie."

Across the road we'd go with a skip and a run, full of joy and excitement to help our neighbour. We sometimes fetched *cippeens* – kindling – to help her light her fire. She used old newspapers soaked in paraffin oil and a bundle of *cippeens* to get it started. We also brought her fresh milk from our farm. Mum often did these chores when the need arose. When we were finished helping her, she gave us currant buns and tea, and the three of us sat at the table chatting. Most often, we pestered her to tell us stories about her life in America.

Danjoe made sure that she had sufficient turf to keep her home warm. He neatly stacked it at one gable of her cottage. She also depended on him to get her medication anytime he was in the nearest big town, which he gladly collected for her.

I often heard her say, "Bleh-shew, Danjoe."

Otherwise, our lovely neighbour was self-sufficient, as she was well able to cook. In her big open-hearth fireplace, she burned turf, which heated her living room to a modest degree. Over the fire stood a black cast-iron crane with hooks. She hung her black kettle and her three-legged pot on it, including other cooking vessels, all made from cast iron. The crane was movable in different directions, and allowed her to cook meat, cabbage, potatoes, and bake bread for daily sustenance.

Her fire was also used for drying and airing clothes, especially during wintertime. A clothesline for this purpose was strung across the wall above the fireplace.

In one corner of her living room, an eggshell-blue dresser stood proud. It was a humble piece of furniture – the fitted kitchen of rural Ireland in years gone by. The main function of the shelved top part, with glass doors, was for displaying willow-pattern Delftware. Sugar, flour, and milk were stored underneath the shelves, and a large white enamel jug stood here, where Mrs O'Brien stored money, important letters, and oddments.

In the middle section, a multitude of curios was stored in two drawers, the contents of which interested me the most: little china dolls, tiny teddy bears, and postcards; sewing buttons, pens and pencils, and much more. I would spend hours turning them over and examining each one. To my sheer delight, she allowed me to take some home at times.

She would say, "Maggie, darlin', take that home with you, I don't need it."

In some thatched cottages and other farmhouses in rural Ireland back then, the dresser was also known to house a hatching hen, in the lower half. This was the safest place for her to hatch her eggs, to protect them from predatory animals. The broody hen sat on the eggs, on a bed of straw in the comfort of the dresser, for twenty-one days. Once her chicks nibbled at the inside of the eggs and emerged, the woman of the house hand-reared them until they were old enough to be housed in the hen house or coop outside.

While Mrs O'Brien didn't have any hens, she stored other household items, such as pots and pans, basins, and old crockery in the lower half of the dresser.

She must have been a talented crafter in her younger days because her modest home was beautifully decorated with all sorts of handmade cushions, chair throws, and small hand-painted pictures, which hung on the dusty pink walls of each room.

I will never forget the beautiful multi-coloured patchwork quilt that covered her black cast-iron bed – a work of art, handknitted by herself. Beside her bed stood an old wooden chair. Tears soaked her handkerchief as she told Ted and me that the old photo hanging on the wall above the chair was of her parents, who had passed on years ago.

Her cottage was rectangular, divided into three rooms, with each one occupying the full width of the house, but it had no central hallway. First there was the kitchen, with a door leading into bedroom one. If I had to fetch something for her from bedroom two, I had to walk through the first bedroom and open a door into the second one.

I remember Mum making regular visits to her in the evenings. With the aid of a Tilley lamp, they chatted about health matters, flowers, and local news. The lamp had a wick, burned paraffin, and provided a warm white light for their cosy evening chats. Mum told me that before she left to return home from her visit to our lovely neighbour, she always said, "Bye, bye, see you again very soon, Mrs O'Brien."

And she always replied with, "Goodnight, Kate, the grace of God be upon you."

On Sunday evenings, our lovely neighbour was particularly benevolent, as she facilitated the playing of a local game called handball, which required a large wall, such as the gable end of her house. The players, including Pop and Grandpa, gathered every Sunday evening at her gable end, which faced the roadway, and played handball against it for a few hours. The competition in these games sometimes got heated, with shouts, roars, and laughter. They bounced that ball off the road and, using their hands as a bat, whacked it off the wall, always trying to trick their opponents. The teams of players were known locally as the crowd that played handball.

They appreciated her kindness and she enjoyed the fun and laughter she heard through the back wall of her kitchen, while she sat by her fire. This was one of the occasions it was necessary for her to tug at her headscarf and pull it behind her somewhat deaf ear, so she could better hear the joviality of the handball players.

Mum and Danjoe, through the kindness of their hearts, generally took care of Mrs O'Brien, but there was a dilemma in the event that she became extremely ill and they couldn't meet her needs anymore. After an episode or two of her feeling poorly, they discussed what would become of her. And I heard them make a solemn promise that they would never agree to their lovely neighbour being admitted to a County Home.

County Homes were founded in the early 1920s, after the formation of the Irish Free State, and there was one in every county in the Republic of Ireland. They were institutions for the elderly and infirm, including chronic and long-term cases. They provided hospital care, midwifery, homed unmarried mothers, and acted as fever hospitals for infectious diseases. In the 1940s and '50s, poverty and TB were rife in rural Ireland, and in County Kerry in particular. Hence it was generally known that the scariest words an elderly person could hear was the mention of a County Home. The care in these establishments was substandard, and Mum and Danjoe were adamant that Mrs O'Brien would not suffer this fate.

What an amazing change of lifestyle for her, from living in the United States of America, to residing in a little thatched cottage in rural Ireland. While the trauma of the burglary may have stayed with her, I remember her being a pleasant elderly lady, who was forever grateful for any act of kindness that came her way.

Our Cow Herd

It is possible that humans may think cows are not intelligent and do not have feelings but ponder this from one having spent a lifetime in the company of cows!

On our little farm between the mountains and the sea, we kept seven or eight cows that provided the bulk of our family income. Invariably, their calves arrived in the world at night-time and most were sold to support our household expenditure. During calving time, no sleep was had by either Pop or Grandpa as they played midwife, making sure all went well with the birthing. They tended to the animals, with light from a metal-framed glass lamp with a wick which burned paraffin. It had a handle for carrying and for hanging it up in the barn.

While we had electricity in our home for kitchen and room lights only, our farm sheds didn't have power. When electrification first became available in Gorse Valley in the late 1940s and the early 1950s, people worried that they couldn't afford it, so they used it sparingly.

On the occasion when I had to say a final goodbye to a calf before they were taken to the fair, tears welled in my eyes, as I always got attached to them. I remember the morning our white calf with black spots was destined to go. It was too much for me, and I ran way up to the far end of the grazing field, sat on a boulder, and tears flowed down my face like a river escaping a dam. I'm sure Ted felt sorrowful, too, as these wide-eyed, joyful, cuddly creatures were our pets.

Along with selling the calves, we sold milk the cows produced to the creamery. Pop's mood always lifted when the postman arrived with his fat cheque payment from the creamery for milk supplied.

Just like the calves, our cows were like pets – we knew them all by name – and each one in turn responded when called. Beneath each of their furred frames lay a beating heart, a nervous system, and intelligence. Not human intelligence, no, but still a clear intelligence. Gazing into their wide eyes, they exuded a sort of peace and tranquillity that brought about a connection and togetherness with us their human family.

Ted's cow Gertie was a special breed, a Kerry Cow, an agile beast that could happily live on rough mountain terrain. As black as soot, with slender white horns and wide docile eyes, she appeared to yearn for human company, most always Ted's. He returned this and loyalty in spades.

Some households, in County Kerry in particular, though they were not farmers, would keep a Kerry Cow. Having only a tiny plot of land, or maybe just a haggard, they kept their little cow to supply their household milk needs. Their wee cow, known for her calm temperament and being easy to keep and manage, became more like their pet, and most always grew close to her owners.

Mabel, my cow, was roan-coloured – red and white – and had wide brown eyes. And while she had a bulky frame, underneath lay a placid personality. Mabel always amazed me with her ability to sleep while standing. Long backrubs and chewing her cud were her favourite things. When out in pasture, Gertie and Mabel always gravitated towards each other, having developed a close bond from the time they were young calves.

Milking time on our farm was like clockwork – a kind of military-style manoeuvre. It had to be done at seven o'clock each morning and again at six o'clock each evening. Otherwise, the cows might feel uncomfortable, and milk would leak from their udders.

Springtime's arrival sometimes caused a dilemma because, when left out to pasture after spending months indoors, they became a little wild. They were full of the joys of spring, running, jumping, and munching on the sweet-smelling grass. It is the time of year when cows are most happy. But to round them up and get them back indoors was next to impossible – much like prisoners being returned to jail, they didn't want to be confined to the four walls of their shed again. However, they soon learned that being indoors was temporary, and when milking time was finished, they would be free to roam the pastures once more.

Some cows were a bit tetchy and giddy while being milked and could give you a rap of their stinky, dung-ridden tail in the face. Or maybe lash out with a quick kick of a hind leg, knocking you off balance. But, lucky for Ted and me, our cows Gertie and Mabel had a quiet and calm nature. We pulled on their teats with all our might, until our galvanised buckets were full to the brim with frothy white milk. This chore was carried out twice each day, come hell or high water.

One particular cow in our herd, Pop's Bessie, broke the mould. Our mum milked three or four of the other cows, all the while calming them by singing sweet tunes. Pop had the honour of milking Bessie, and he didn't sing to her. No, she tested what little patience he possessed beyond breaking point, as she was a daft, tetchy, and nervous cow. Perhaps she wasn't right in the head. The cowshed was partitioned off, with each cow having their own wooden stall. It was rare that she would go into her own one without creating havoc amongst the rest of the herd. Instead, she went across the small cowshed into another cow's cubicle and devoured the food from her trough. It was almost impossible to coax her back to her own place, as the other cows' feed was also high on her agenda.

Even when back in situ, she was hyper and couldn't stand still for a second. She would lash out with nasty kicks that often times sent Pop, his milking bucket and his three-legged wooden stool flying across the shed, splattering milk everywhere. Having enough of her outbursts and red-faced with anger, he'd spansel her. The spansel, a piece of thick rope, was tied tight around her hind legs, restricting her movements. He could then milk her, though with some trepidation.

Our cows usually calved in March each year. While this was a joyous time, as each adorable calf was born, it could also be sad. On the odd occasion, one of our cows would deliver a stillborn calf. I sobbed as I watched a perfect little calf, still wet and slimy, lying lifeless beside Mama cow on a bed of straw. The distress of the cow at these times was profound, evidenced through her cries and forlorn demeanour. Ted's downcast eyes were proof of his heartbreak too.

Lo and behold, it was Bessie's turn to give birth. She obliged with a lovely calf, roan-coloured like herself, and we named him Harry. Bessie lowed with pride while licking her offspring all over. Harry's tail wagged at a furious pace as the beastings – Bessie's first milk – frothed and dripped from his pap-filled mouth.

"Let's go and see how Harry is getting on, Maggie," Ted often said.

"Okay," I would answer, "we haven't seen him in a while."

Bessie and Harry's bond strengthened over the coming months and she nourished her calf while they were together in the barn. Once Harry was strong enough, they got to spend time in the pasture, always by each other's side. If another cow from the herd came within a hair's breadth of Harry, Bessie would furiously puck her away. Over time, Harry learned from his mother that he, too, could eat grass, and as a result became a little less dependent on her.

Then the time came for Harry to be sold. He was about five months old now, a bulky fellow, and bucking about the place with boundless energy. Pop had just left the back yard with his prized calf on the back of a borrowed pick-up truck. All of a sudden, Bessie bolted from the cowshed and took after them like a shot out of a gun. She butted the side of the truck with her horns, bellowing up at Harry. Not making any progress in halting the truck, she had another go, this time butting it so hard that she nearly turned it over.

Pop put the boot down on the accelerator and the truck powered forward, leaving Bessie on the side of the road, pining at the loss of her beautiful calf. She returned to our farm, agitated and distressed. Poor heartbroken Bessie lowed and moaned for several days afterwards, looking everywhere for Harry. The other cows would sometimes vocalise along with her, as they too were aware of her loss.

Through this experience, we can frame the reality that cows have intelligence and feelings. Their relationship within a herd and with humans' points to them being sentient beings – amazing creatures, aware of events going on around them, and often reacting emotionally to circumstances good and bad.

Our Equine Family

Equines have a rich history as the real-life heroes of agriculture, and as members of this family, our Neddy, Blackie, and Bobby were very much in this league. It was a pure joy to spend my childhood days in their company, but a noble steed one was not inclined to be!

Neddy's coat was an even mixture of beige and brown, with a wide black stripe stretched along his spine and down his shoulders, known as the Donkey's Cross. This natural marking on donkeys' backs is believed by some to have been passed down genetically through history. Others believe it has religious significance.

When Ted and I entered their grazing field behind the haggard, our donkey pointed his long ears forward and, with a sad drooping face, it was like he was inviting us to come closer and pet him. Which, of course, we always did. We loved all our equines, but we had enormous affection for Neddy. He was the highlight of our younger days, and we loved the bones of him. But he had a mind of his own, and there were times when he could be immensely sulky.

While Neddy's trip to the creamery was an everyday occurrence, he was like a part-time worker – he didn't like being disturbed or having to exert himself in any way. His ideal lifestyle was grazing in the lush pastures of the paddock.

Most days, we would pay particular attention to him, giving him big hugs, long ear rubs, and a juicy carrot or two from the vegetable patch. Sometimes, and unknown to Pop, we snuck him a few handfuls of oats.

We often put on his bridle and took bareback rides on him. As far as I was concerned, Neddy was going to one day win the Cheltenham Gold Cup, but this particular day he was having none of it. He connived his way to an opening in the hedge of the grazing paddock, with me on his back. It led to a dry embankment he knew well, as he liked to shelter there to avoid the sweltering summer sun.

Neddy stood still like a plank of wood and wouldn't budge an inch, even though I tried with all my might to get him to move, giving him a little prod with the heels of my wellington boots. I even jolted the reins a few times, but no way was he going to move. On my last attempt to get him to shift his bulky body, he retaliated. Bucking and kicking out with his hind legs, he sent me flying into the air. I hurtled less than gracefully over the top of his head and landed, smack bang in the middle of a bunch of briars and nettles.

Crying like the rain, my heart thundering, I ran out the paddock gate and into our farmyard. Ted heard my cries and ran to my assistance.

"Maggie, why are you crying? What happened to you?"

"It was Neddy. He threw me right into a bunch of briars and nettles."

Ted knew that broad-leafed, dark-green plants grew beside bunches of nettles – dock leaves, believed to have curing properties for nettle stings.

"I'll grab some dock leaves to take the sting away."

"Hurry back, Ted, my hands and legs are burning."

He rubbed the stings on my hands and legs, chanting, "Docky leaf, docky leaf, take the sting of the nettles away."

But the dock leaves didn't work. He put his arms around me, and we scampered to the kitchen, where we told Mum my tale of woe. She washed my cuts and scrapes, then rubbed cream on them, including the nettle stings. Soothing Germolene antiseptic cream, the healing aroma of which always made me feel better.

"Off you go now, my darlings. Forget about Neddy for today and have some fun playing outdoors."

"Okay, Mum, we will," we said in unison.

As already mentioned, our pony Blackie pulled our trap to take us to Mass on Sunday. Some ponies or horses can get upset and uneasy if something startles them. Maybe the rattle of their harness chains or if a bird flies past them. They will often kick out or rear up. But not our little pony, she was steadfast and cooperative at all times. She did the lesser in-between tasks on our farm, such as drawing turf from the bog.

Bobby, our horse, was a powerful, athletic animal – chestnut brown, with a beautiful long mane and a blaze of white from the top of his forehead to his nose. A gentle giant, similar to Danjoe's horse Molly, he had four white hairy fetlocks. He was even-tempered and plodded along regardless of whether he was ploughing, pulling a cart, or doing other tough work on the farm.

Grandpa often surprised Ted and me when he was finished working with Bobby in the fields. They would arrive back to our farmyard, tired, after he and Bobby had ploughed the last furrow in preparation for sowing the potatoes. With his wellington boots and his horse's white fetlocks covered with muddy earth from the field, he'd throw us up high on Bobby's back. Ted up front, held onto the horse hames and I held on behind, my arms around my brother's waist. Led by Grandpa, Bobby moved back to his stable at a slow pace, and we thoroughly enjoyed our jaunt on his muscular back.

Bobby bedded down for the night in the company of Neddy and Blackie. In the late evening, the two of us often peeped over the half door of their stable, and it was delightful to hear them munching their hay in the warmth of their stall. Last thing at night, Grandpa went to their stable and, by the light of his lamp, checked them to make sure they were okay before he went to bed.

In late spring, our equines grazed in the lush two-acre paddock at the back of our farm buildings and got along the finest. They had a dry dusty patch in the centre of the paddock, and took great delight rolling in this particular spot, as it helped them to get rid of any flies or mites that irritated their skin. At first, they would paw at the spot to loosen the dirt, then they rolled over from one side to the other several times, their legs pawing the air. Having finished their rolling activity, they jumped up on all fours, shook their heads and tails, sneezed, then sauntered off, delighted that their daily rolling session was complete. It was natural for them to take a daily dunk in the dust during spring and dry summer weather.

The only other company they had in the paddock was an age-old raggedy white-haired goat called Maisy. Having long crooked horns and only one eye, her sideways glance was scary. She was happy, though, chewing hay from an old rusty oil barrel. Unlike her companions, this was the toughest work she had to endure in any one day.

Grandpa made sure our equines were well cared for. He always checked that their grazing paddock was free from *geosadáns* – poisonous ragwort – digging them up with a spade and disposing of them with care. I remember how he painstakingly clipped Bobby's coat with a hand clippers in October each year, when his winter coat had fully grown. Having oiled it first, he started behind his ears and worked midway down his belly, clipping him with care. Horses grow thicker coats in winter to protect them from chilly weather but, because Bobby was kept indoors in the warmth of his stable at this time of year, Grandpa clipped him, allowing him to have an even body temperature.

On regular occasions, Grandpa took Neddy, Blackie, and Bobby to the local forge to have their hooves trimmed and steel shoes fitted. My brother and I often watched as Tomo the Farrier, wearing a leather apron, trimmed and shod our animals. It was fascinating to watch this craftsman at work.

After trimming their hooves, he would bring out steel shoes and fit them for size. These shoes were shaped and moulded in a burning-hot furnace. Then, back at his workbench, he'd adjust them on the anvil with a hammer. Once satisfied that each shoe was a perfect fit, he fitted them with special nails to our equines' hoofs.

Our grandfather discouraged Pop from handling Neddy or Blackie at all times, as he was more or less devoid of patience for them. If Pop attempted to bridle Neddy for some work he needed him to do, our donkey galloped at speed to the other end of the grazing field, where he'd glare back at Pop, with nostrils dilated and ruffled mane.

Blackie also seemed to be aware of Pop's impatience. Even though she was normally a well-behaved pony, she acted up in Pop's presence, bucking and kicking her hind legs in the air. Their behaviour indicated unease when Pop was about.

While Neddy epitomized the saying 'as stubborn as a donkey', my brother and I adored him. Our three equines were much loved and of the utmost importance to us. We would not have been without any one of them on our farm holding. Even when Pop bought a state-of-the-art tractor to make farming life easier, Grandpa was adamant that Neddy, Blackie, and Bobby would remain on our farm until the day each one of them drew their last breath.

Sally, Our Dog

Our little dog Sally's depth of intelligence was astounding. While she was a perfect herding dog who thrived when working or challenged, she was special to me, and indeed to Ted too.

Sally was black, with a blaze of white on her muzzle, neck, and legs. Being a collie breed, she never went anywhere upright, preferring to creep along, low to the ground. She had an intense stare, or 'eye', used to calculate how best to herd and control our sheep or indeed any of our animals.

Come nightfall, and when she had scoffed her dinner, Sally made her bed in the open turf shed. It suited her to perfection, as she disliked being confined indoors. She bedded down on a flattened sack of hay, right beside the stack of turf. And she didn't just plop down any old way – she circled many times. Sometimes, she even appeared to do a circle dance before settling into her bed, still ever watchful.

If a neighbour's cat came prowling at night, Sally's hackles went into overdrive. She would freeze, stare, the hairs on her neck and back rising. At this stage, the cat needed a way out, and fast. After weighing up her possibilities, she hightailed it through the hedge, her ears back, with Sally leaping and bounding behind her.

Worse still, a fox sometimes came preying on Mum's hens and tried to grab one – a dinner for herself and her growing cub litter. But not on Sally's watch. She could detect Mrs Fox's scent from miles away. Once the fox poked her nose within the boundary of our farmyard, she received the same welcome as the cat, only more intense.

At the break of day, and without fail, Sally sat outside our back door, her eyes focused and her ears pointing skywards, ready and alert for a signal to begin her working day.

Our flock of sheep – numbering about fifty, including their lambs in springtime – were scattered far and wide on the hillside. These Blackface, hardy and horned upland sheep, were bred to tolerate cold, rough mountainous terrain. Pop, aided by Sally, needed to gather them up and bring them back to our farm for annual shearing, branding, and dipping.

Mountainside gathering of sheep could be a hazardous one for Pop and Sally. A dense fog could come in fast, impairing their sight and judgement, and they would have to wait for many hours until it cleared up. These perilous conditions were always on Pop's mind before he set out on this endeavour.

One particular time Pop chose to gather our sheep from the mountains happened to be a balmy mid-summer day. Having had years of experience of mountainous dangers, he always held a stick, with a knob at the top. He swished and prodded it as he walked, clearing his way and detecting any soft spots on the heathery ground in which he could twist his ankle. His blackthorn stick, known for its hardness and durability, was important to him, and one he carefully cut from a tree near our home. It was his main safety implement.

While gathering the sheep, Pop's face turned beet red and sweaty, as rounding up his free-roaming flock was demanding work. Sally's tongue hung out, beating like a drum as she panted for breath. But she didn't falter. She listened for Pop's many whistle signals and obeyed his every command throughout the entire day. Crouching low, she crept alongside the sheep and rounded them in a circle, as commanded.

Disaster struck when one of the sheep stumbled and fell into a boggy hole. Pop took hold of her crooked horns and dragged her to safety. When he examined her, he found one of her legs was severely injured. Scratching his head in bewilderment, he had no idea what to do. The sun would soon fade, and he knew he had to act fast. Meanwhile, Sally took complete charge of the other sheep, keeping them in a tight circle.

All of a sudden, Pop thought of something that may help. He grabbed a small stick, and with the aid of one of his socks, splinted the sheep's leg. She hobbled a bit and then some more, and they continued their homeward journey, though at a much slower pace.

After what seemed like an eternity, the sheep, accompanied by Pop and Sally, arrived back on our farm. As he tended to the injured animal's leg, he told us all about what happened during the long stressful and laborious day on the hillside.

The backbreaking work of shearing and branding of each sheep began in earnest the next day. Once the shearing was finished, Pop opened a gallon of both blue and red paint. Smiling big and wide, he painted his initials across the back of each sheep. The branding of our flock in this way was to identify them in the event that they got mixed with another farmer's flock when they were returned to the heathered landscape.

Bringing the sheep back to the mountainside was a much easier task for Pop and Sally. They drove the flock up the boreen, then on to a heathery grazing spot about halfway up the hillside and set them free.

On each occasion when the sheep were sheared, their wool was sorted and put into large grain sacks and sold at the market a few townlands away. Farming communities back then were truly resourceful. To earn a crust and add to the depleting family budget, they sold sheep's wool, goose feathers, eggs, and maybe a calf or some pigs.

The same rounding up of the sheep began again in early autumn, when they were brought home from the hills for dipping. Sally, as always, was at the ready and did her duty diligently.

This time of year, was exciting, as neighbours got together, including Danjoe, for the annual plunge-dipping of their sheep. While it was challenging work for the men, catching and dipping well over 150 bleating sheep, there was an air of camaraderie about it.

Ted and I, including neighbouring children, buzzing with excitement, watched from the wall of the dipping pen as each sheep got their annual bath. Sally sat close by - eyes glued to the sheep and ready to herd them back to their holding pen should any try to escape.

A long pole called a dipping stick, with a cast-iron crook at one end, was used to keep each sheep submerged in the dipping solution for a brief time, with only their heads peeping up. Their woolly coats got a complete soaking, which protected them from infestation of external parasites, and they were released to roam the mountainside later in the evening.

One day, to our great surprise, Pop arrived home with a new dog he had got from an elderly man named Tom, who lived two townlands away. Mum couldn't believe it.

"Jimmy, why in the name of the man above did you get a new dog? We already have Sally, the best dog in the world."

"Tom is feeling very poorly," Pop replied. "He can't take care of him and begged me to take the dog home with me."

Our new dog, an undisciplined mongrel named Bran, was brindle, with one icy-blue eye, and one brown one, which made him appear strange. My brother and I patted him on the head and he gazed up at us, sitting on his back legs, tongue hanging out, with a Cheshire Cat smile on his face.

Sally was none too pleased with the newcomer, and snarled at him if he ventured too close to her.

Even though he was well past puppy stage, Bran was excitable, unruly, and disobedient. He leaped and bounded about the place and was a tad bonkers in the head, chasing the cats and attacking the hens. Worse, though, he scoffed food from the kitchen table, and barked incessantly day and night. Many attempts to get him to sit still for a second and moderate his behaviour failed miserably.

To try and calm him, Pop fetched a light log of wood, fixed a piece of rope to it and tied it around his neck. It dangled between his front legs, causing him to walk awkwardly, and limiting his movement. After about six weeks of wearing the wooden contraption, he calmed down and Pop removed it.

My big brother and I became fond of Bran and taught him new tricks like 'give me the paw' as well as 'fetch and roll over'. We gave him water and food daily and showered him with love. He was our pet, too, and he followed us almost everywhere.

One day, unbeknown to anyone, he bounded out of our farm gate. We heard a loud bang and, panic-stricken, Mum; Ted and I ran out.

The driver of a motorcar, the only vehicle that passed by our house that day, looked at us. "Really, really sorry. Your dog ran straight out in front of my car."

"It's okay," Mum replied, "it wasn't your fault."

Poor Bran staggered back into our haggard and lay down beside a wildflower bed. A short while later, all life ebbed from his body and he closed his eyes forever. While I was glad that he didn't have any visible injury, I can still remember that dreadful day, as if it were yesterday. Bran's sudden passing will be forever etched in my memory, and Ted often mentions it too.

Sally didn't appear to miss Bran and continued to make sure the animals she rounded up and herded knew their place. It was her natural instinct to gather, herd, and protect all livestock on our farm, but particularly so our sheep that grazed on the mountainside. She undertook her duties in her quiet and faultless way, and we have enduring memories of her as a constant in our childhood years.

A Hive of Activity

My brother and I had never a need to visit a zoo, for we had one in our own backyard, including species of all different shapes and sizes. It was a joy to see how they all interacted with each other, and our farmyard was a hive of activity, colour, and sound.

Neddy, Bobby, and Blackie sometimes peered over the paddock gate in the hope of getting a treat like a crunchy, juicy home-grown carrot. Their goat companion was too laid back, munching hay, to mutter a sound.

A clowder of feral ginger cats and their *piscíns* – kittens – did their own thing in the hay barn, some running around trying to catch mice and rats and some sitting, purring to their heart's delight following a feast of the same rodents.

Mum's hens were multi-coloured and mixed breeds such as White Leghorns, Rhode Island Reds, small speckled-grey Bantams, and one white and grey Frizzle – wherever she hailed from, I can't remember. After laying an egg, each one felt it necessary to proclaim the good news. They paraded around, emitting high-pitched clucking sounds for all to hear.

And, of course, there was beady eyed Mr Cockerel, also a Rhode Island Red, shuffling around the farmyard, thinking he was the boss, shrilling and crowing at all times of the day, especially at the break of dawn. Betty, our ginger cat, was petrified of him. If they had a close encounter, she arched her back, fearing he would attack her with his long talons, but she mostly gave him a wide berth. While our rooster thought he was the boss of the farmyard, Sally upstaged him, as she was the Managing Director.

Hilda, the only remaining white-feathered duck out of a family of eight, quacked and waddled amongst the hens, and enjoyed her daily swim in a swampy pond, created by rainfall. I remember, when she got too frail to walk, carrying her tucked under my arm, with her neck stretched forth, to her feeding bowl full of oats and boiled potatoes, which she ate at a snail's pace.

When not out in pasture, our cows and calves mooed from their sheds, and unless a restless one escaped, they didn't pay much attention or bother any of the other animals. They varied in colour, from black to white-spotted and roan.

An aviary of birds sang sweetly from the old oak tree overlooking our farmyard, and noisy cawing crows swooped down over the many animal feeding vessels at every opportunity to steal a morsel of food.

And then there was mama pig, snorting and grunting in the pigsty. Almost all new arrivals were born on our farm in springtime and soon fitted into regular farm proceedings. But mama pig did not oblige and could give birth during any month of the year.

She was the mama who caused havoc when her bonhams – piglets – arrived, as she was capable of sitting on one or two of them, squashing them to death with her hefty body. During the first few days after their birth, it was necessary for Pop and Grandpa to do round-the-clock surveillance of mama pig to protect her young. While she was settling down to rest, they would push the bonhams out of her way with a farmyard brush. She was a grumpy old sod and they could not personally handle the bonhams, as this angered her. But then it was hard to blame her being crotchety – a litter of twelve wriggling piglets in one go was a tall order for any mother, stretching her maternal instincts to their limits.

Mama pig prepared her birthing bed well in advance of the arrival of her offspring. She chopped up fresh golden straw with her sharp teeth and arranged it into shape, pawing it with her front feet until satisfied it was comfortable. Once she was ready, she nestled into her bed, as she needed much peace and quiet for several days preceding the birth of her babies.

After several hours of excruciating labour pains, her cute pink-skinned bonhams arrived one after the other. Sometimes, a weak bonham came out, being the runt of the litter. This piglet needed extra special care, being hand-fed milk with a bottle and teat, similar to that of a newborn baby. Mum and Nano gladly undertook that task in the kitchen, keeping their guest warm by the fire, in a tea chest.

When feeding time arrived, mama pig grunted and groaned loudly, a signal for her litter to feed. They snuggled up to her, fed with gusto, and afterwards snoozed away. It only took a few days after birth for them to learn to stay out of Mama's way when she needed to lay down to rest. In time, the runt of the litter could leave the care of Mum and Nano and join family members in the pigsty.

One time, a certain little piglet could not return to his family. During the time he stayed in our home, my brother and I adored him. When he outgrew the tea chest, he ran around our kitchen like a dog or cat and scurried in and out between the table and chair legs. He became too domesticated to live with his natural family and we named him Malachy.

Grandpa built a separate wee shed for him attached to the back of our farmhouse. Ted and I fed him daily and fluffed up his bed of straw. Though still small for his age, he scoffed every morsel of food from his wooden trough. Malachy was a rather clean pig and kept his bed and toilet place separate. We mucked out his shed every second day with shovels and an old wooden wheelbarrow.

Sally was a bit dubious of Malachy in the beginning but warmed to him after a while and watched Ted and me play with him daily. One day, Ted was playing rough and tumble with Malachy and their fun got too high spirited. With his sharp teeth, Malachy tore a gaping hole in the leg of Ted's pants. I jumped up and down laughing, but Ted was not amused, as he had to bear the sad news about his pants to Mum.

Killing a pig was a major event in Gorse Valley and had to be done in the colder months of the year, as refrigerators were unheard of in the area. And because the produce – bacon, black pudding, and sausages – were shared with neighbours, planning the event was of the utmost importance, so everyone could benefit over a longer period of time.

Sadly, the time arrived for Malachy's demise, a horrific day for Ted and me. We ran to Ada's house, as we couldn't bear to witness the event. Pop did the dastardly deed, helped by reluctant Grandpa, as he too didn't want to be part of Malachy's passing.

Our kitchen became a hive of activity. Mum and Nano made black puddings and sausages, filling the entrails with a mix of meat, oats, and breadcrumbs. Pop and Grandpa cut up the meat into portions, salted them in a large wooden barrel, and hung the pieces for our own consumption up in the lean-to shed to be cured. I well recall how fatty parts of the animal's abdomen were also cut up, rendered for lard and stored in large cream and tan earthenware pots for later use.

As was customary, a day or two later, Mum and Nano, accompanied by me, took some of the meat, sausages, and black pudding around to share with our neighbours, to their delight.

My brother and I had become particularly fond of Malachy and would have loved to have kept him, as we did every animal on the farm. Ted was heartbroken about our pet pig's demise and could not bring himself to eat bacon for several years afterwards. My soft-hearted brother, one of the qualities that endeared me to him.

Keeping all of the animals fed and watered was almost a fulltime job for family members, excluding Cait and Elizabeth, as they had no interest in them. A massive pot of potatoes was boiled daily, as the basic food for most. The pig ate what we called 'pig slop', a mixture of potatoes, skimmed milk, leftover bread, and vegetable peels. The bonhams feasted on this same mixture when weaned. Apart from foraging in the haggard and outdoors for seeds, grains, and insects, the cockerel, hens, and solitary duck got 'hens' mess', similar to the pig food, but a drier mixture. Once they were about eight weeks old, the chickens ate the same.

When not outdoors, our equines munched hay from their stalls, joined by their goat friend. The cows munched hay from their stalls, too, and sometimes got a treat of bran and mash to improve their milk yield. Their calves only got to suckle from their mother's milk for a short time, and when weaned they drank skimmed milk. They eventually went on to eat the same food as the cows. Sally got leftover dinner and a small portion of meat from our main family meal. Fresh water was drawn from the nearby well in buckets, for all as needed.

My parents and grandparents often grumbled about the endless rain, mists, and winds that engulfed Gorse Valley, particularly so during winter – a time of the year they thought came in too soon and stayed too long. It hindered them greatly in their efforts to care for our animals, dragging feed and fodder here there and everywhere.

Apart from when an animal was sold or killed, necessary for survival at that time, I was truly blessed to live amongst a zoo of farm animals in my childhood. To be amongst these animals at any time of day was pleasurable, but it was delightful to hear their amazing dawn chorus on a mid-summer morning.

A Tea Chest

Tea chests are plywood crates that have been used for centuries for the transportation of loose tea around the world. But Ted and I found a rather unusual use for one.

During the early 1950s in rural Ireland, and I'm sure for many years beforehand, empty tea chests were never disregarded. Sometimes, they were used as playpens for toddlers, or baby chicks were kept in them.

Other times, an undernourished, orphaned lamb or sickly bonham was nursed back to health beside the open fire in the kitchen. It was usually the woman of the farmhouse – in our case, Mum, helped by Nano – who undertook this work. They would bottle-feed the sickly creatures with milk until they were strong and well enough to join the rest of the animals on the farm.

The two of us often played around the yard when we didn't have chores to do. Some days, we played a game of catch, or maybe hide and seek. Goodness knows, we had a multitude of places to hide and never again be found.

Other days, we would sit up high on the haystack, in the barn, with our legs dangling, catching warm rays of the sun. Some years earlier, Nano received the most amazing rainbow-coloured wool in a parcel from our Aunt Maureen in America. It was the most used hank of wool ever. My brother and I would knit a purse or little narrow scarf with it. The next day, or maybe a few days later, we would rip our knitted pieces asunder, then start over and knit something else in a new and wondrous design that we thought would look amazing.

Our gurry hen – a hen in broody mode – had sat on ten eggs for twenty-one days, always observed by Mum. There were twelve eggs in the nest originally to be hatched out, but on Mum's close inspection, holding them up to the light while rattling them, she discovered that two of them were *gliogars*, meaning they did not contain chicks. Mum chucked both eggs out of the nest, as it was a useless exercise for the hen to sit on them.

The incubation time was complete, and a brood of ten fluffy yellow chicks emerged from the eggs. Mum couldn't wait until all ten chickens matured at about twenty-two weeks and begin to produce their first eggs.

But Mum had to keep a close watch on Betty, as baby chickens were a tempting meal for our semi-feral feline. She made sure the cat was housed indoors, in the cowshed at nighttime, and once daylight broke, Mum chased her to the far end of the haggard. Our gurry hen was also on high alert. If she saw Betty with a side eye, she lunged and flew at her and gave her some nasty pecks on her rear end, sending her back where she came from.

One particular day, there was mischief in our heads, and we abandoned our knitting projects and other pastimes. We had just noticed Mum's chickens, who were on the brink of laying their first eggs, busily pecking the ground here and there around the hay barn. We gave chase, caught a few, and put them in a tea chest. Seconds later, they flapped their wings and flew out of the wooden box.

"This is great fun," Ted said. "Let's see how many chickens we can fit in the tea chest.

"Okay, Ted," I said, and we scampered around the hay barn, catching and bundling chickens in our arms. The chickens were skittish, squawking, and flapping their wings, trying to escape and deter us from catching them. Sally took immense pleasure in helping us round them up. Obviously, they must have annoyed her on a number of occasions, as it appeared that she disliked them. With her help, we kept going until we had all ten of Mum's beautiful, white-feathered chickens in the tea chest, with the lid shut tight. Just then I remembered Mrs O'Brien. "Ted, we're late, we need to do chores for Mrs O'Brien."

"Let's go now, Maggie, and we can come back and release Mum's chickens when we are finished."

We hurried and did Mrs O'Brien's chores and she gave us tea and buns. Her little dog Toby was looking for some attention and we played fetch with him for a while.

On returning home, we grabbed Neddy's halter and paid our daily visit to him in the paddock. We tried to halter him, testing our luck to see whether he was in a cooperative mood to be ridden or not, but he wasn't having any of it and galloped like a bolt of lightning to the far end of the paddock. He stood in the distance, gaping back at us with a wild look on his face and a ruffled mane. This was our answer: stay away from me today, you two, I am having a day of leisure.

We ran indoors, where Mum was singing in soprano voice while washing some clothes in the galvanised bathtub in the kitchen. We were only too happy to help her. Our Mum's poor wrinkled hands were testament to the hardship she endured. But she delighted in pegging the clothes on a lengthy line, held up by two wooden poles in the haggard, where they were crisply dried by the four winds.

All of a sudden, Mum turned to us. "Ted and Maggie, have you two seen my chickens anywhere?"

We looked at each other, dumbfounded, having forgotten to release the chickens from the tea chest.

"Come, Mum, come," Ted said, his voice meek."

We rushed to the tea chest where we had confined the chickens. But Sally got there first, her head tilting while peering at the wooden box. Mum's smile turned upside down, and her head hung low as she discovered that we had unintentionally smothered her ten beautiful, white-feathered chickens.

While she had mature hens that would supply our family with eggs, her poor heart must have been broken at the sight of her lifeless chickens in that tea chest. Her chickens, whose eggs she intended to sell in our local shop, the income of which would buy shoes for us children and household goods. Worse still, the chickens were not fit for human consumption because of the way they died, having been smothered piled together in the tea chest. Sadly, they all had to be buried.

However heartbroken Mum was, she did not utter a cross word to her six-and-seven-year-old scatterbrained son and daughter about the loss of her ten chickens. But Ted was beside himself with fear, dreading what Pop would have to say about the matter.

"Don't be worrying, Ted, all will be fine."

"I hope you are right, Maggie."

Bless our mum, she must have silenced Pop, as he never mentioned the unfortunate tea chest incident.

One of Mum's more important chores each day was bringing in the eggs, bundled in the pocket of her flowery apron. Her laying hens could cause a ruckus, which meant collecting their eggs was an arduous task. Even though the hens had straw-filled laying boxes aplenty in their old shed, they had an annoying habit of laying anywhere other than in the boxes.

They had free range of the farmyard in the daytime, and Mum could find their eggs in a nest in the hay barn, under bushes, in the vegetable patch, or in the flowerbed. Sometimes, they even built a nest in the crevice of the old stone wall at the back of the haggard and laid their eggs there. This was a worthless exercise, as the eggs rolled off the wall and smashed. Myself and my brother always enjoyed helping Mum collect the eggs, during the weekend or when we had a day off school.

Mum forgave us for the 'lost chickens' episode, and we continued to enjoy playing around the farm, and even chasing the hens. The versatility of a tea chest was amazing, and recycling was at its best back then, without people even knowing it, but I would never recommend one for housing chickens.

The Creamery
The creamery and a high-speed donkey escape!

After our cow herd were milked, the fresh creamy milk was taken to the local creamery on a daily basis. The milk they produced early in the morning and the milk yield from the previous evening were taken together in two milk tanks or churns.

When each cow had been milked, the produce was poured from the bucket through a cheesecloth strainer into a scalded tank and the careful straining of the liquid ensured that any impurities were removed. Mum always cleaned and scalded the milk tanks after each use. If this hadn't been done, the stench of sour milk would knock you dead.

During sizzling summer days, the milk tank with the previous evening's milk yield was dunked in our nearby stony stream, to keep the milk cool during the night. There were no modern bulk-milk tanks with built-in cooling systems back then.

The creamery was a designated stand – a platform where full milk tanks were loaded onto – with the square platform made of old planks of wood or mass concrete. It was strategically situated in a townland, convenient for farmers both local and from surrounding areas to bring their milk supplies to.

In rural Ireland, a dairy-disposal company operated a network of travelling creameries to collect milk from farmers, which made remote dairying possible. Lorries equipped with separating and weighing equipment travelled to designated creamery stands to collect milk from these small suppliers.

The lorries had two compartments – one into which the milk from each supplier was poured and measured, with the other separating the cream from the milk. At the creamery stand, the cream was graded and weighed, then recorded in a book with each supplier's name. Afterwards, the skimmed milk was given back to the farmer, which was used to feed the animals, such as pigs and calves, and to make bread at home when it went sour. The cream was taken in the lorries to the Creamery Cooperative, where it was processed into creamy yellow butter.

Our creamery stand was situated at a quaint bridge, beside a grocery shop, and was known as 'The Creamery' to all and sundry.

Grandpa was always the one, along with Neddy, who took the two milk tanks to the creamery each morning. He had been doing this task from the time he was a young boy in short pants. My brother and I always looked forward to days we could go to the creamery with Grandpa.

Neddy was the dutiful animal who made this important journey possible. Like a powerful mini-steam engine, he pulled the donkey cart with the milk tanks onboard, including Grandpa. But the cart was somewhat rickety because of its wheels. The upper square body, including the shafts, were made from oak wood and painted orange. Pop expertly carved and made the round spoked wooden cartwheels, with an axle hub in the middle. But, as rubber was not available in the area at that time, the outer rims of the cartwheels were made of steel by a blacksmith. And the cart didn't have any cushioning springs.

One particular day, we had a day off school and, after a quick breakfast, we helped Grandpa to harness Neddy and yoke him to the cart. Our adventure began when Grandpa commanded Neddy to "Hup now, boy," a signal to begin the journey, and one he understood well. Neddy's ears flicked forward and he picked up pace. We bounced up and down and rattled along, as the steel-rimmed wheels of the cart hit the rough, uneven road. During the journey, and though it was a bumpy ride, both Ted and I had delight in our hearts as we listened to the melodious warbling of the skylarks soaring high above our heads.

The stand was two miles away from our farm, and going there was something of a social occasion. Neighbouring farmers and those from the wider locality made a similar journey and congregated there to deposit their milk supplies. They discussed the weather, the price at cattle fairs, and what they planned to do on their farm that day. On Monday morning, the football matches of the weekend were a central topic of conversation, with all games analysed: who won a particular match and why the other team lost?

With the help of one of the neighbours, Grandpa deposited our milk supply into a large grading and weighing vat. A brief time later, he collected the residual skimmed milk in the tanks and loaded them back onto Neddy's cart.

On this particular morning, we had an extra stop to make, but this was not on Neddy's itinerary. His work schedule was going as far as the creamery each morning and back home, and to travel further than the creamery stand was alien to him. Grandpa had to bring groceries from the shop to his elderly sister, Mary, who lived further along the road. We coaxed Neddy, but no matter how hard we tried he would not budge. No amount of cajoling would get him to move any further.

In the end, we left him there, where he normally waited for his return journey home, and walked the rest of the way to leave the groceries with Grandpa's sister.

When we returned to the creamery stand, Neddy was missing – gone without a trace. Donkeys are stubborn but they are known to be clever. He had left the creamery, still yoked to his cart and with the two tanks half full of skimmed milk onboard and made his way home unaccompanied.

There was no risk from speeding traffic, as there were no motorised vehicles on the roads, but a donkey pulling a cart for two miles on his own must have been a remarkable sight. The clippety-clop of Neddy's hooves hitting the road and the clunking of the steel-rimmed wheels could have raised the dead. It was possible that Neddy encountered obstacles along the way – a stray dog roaming the roads, cows being driven to pasture, or maybe a gaggle of geese – but if any of these difficulties arose, it was clear that he managed to overcome them.

The rest of our family at home could not believe what was happening when Neddy appeared unaccompanied in our backyard. They thought something serious had happened to us. When we arrived home sometime later and explained that he had escaped from the creamery stand, they were astonished.

Later that day, Grandpa was chatting to Danjoe, who had seen Neddy flee the stand.

"I tried to stop him, John, but he was gone at high speed."

"You did your best, man. When that donkey gets an idea into his head, there is no stopping him."

When all calmed down, Ted and I fed the calves and pigs with the skimmed milk, which had survived Neddy's adventure from the creamery stand. This was a chore that both of us liked doing, as the calves and pigs seemed to have a broad smile on their faces when we finished feeding them.

Donkeys like routine and can't be rushed or cajoled into doing something they don't want to do. Neddy's escape plan was a success, and his grassy-hewn paddock awaited, just as he liked it.

Dry Stone Walls

Dry stone walls are a feature of rural Ireland, and they were plentiful in Gorse Valley, criss-crossing in every direction, creating field boundaries similar to that of a green patchwork quilt. Every step my big brother and I took in those unforgettable childhood years, led us through an amazing Lego-like construction of speckled-grey stone walls, guiding us wherever we choose to roam.

The walls are as old as time, built by the strong hands of mountainy farmers. They painstakingly cleared their small fields of stones, which they used to build a boundary wall around their property, thereby creating a more fertile soil for crops and grazing grass to grow within.

No foundation was set, no tool was used to cut the stone, or no mortar to build the walls. Some of the stones were flat and an irregular shape and some were rounded, the latter of which were more difficult to use.

Farmers constructed the walls through careful selection, piling and balancing the stones on top of each other, like a jigsaw puzzle. They built the walls with the largest boulders at the base and the stones getting smaller towards the top. It was a skill handed down from one generation to the next, and the walls were built with stone local to the area, such as limestone, granite or sandstone.

Green moss and ferns grew between the crevices of the walls, which added to their beauty and created a safe haven for small mammals. Farmers in those days had a close connection with the land. They used cow manure in its natural state as fertiliser to grow their crops, and the turf in the boglands was important to them for heating and cooking. As well as that, they respected other aspects of nature and left them be to perform their own natural cycle. Creatures such as insects, snails, birds, and much more were undisturbed, particularly those that sheltered within the stone walls.

Farmers in our townland had a natural tendency to recycle; they improvised and used whatever material was near at hand. New materials were not readily available and were expensive but, nevertheless, the farming community then didn't see the necessity for their use.

Most times, to keep the animals in, they made small gates with wood they found lying around the farm, which had been there for many years. They were hinged to two wooden poles, which were driven into the ground with a sledgehammer between the stone walls. A bolt could be used for opening and closing the gate, but most often a piece of old rope or twine was employed for the same purpose.

I remember many times when there was no entry gate to a field. A small section of the stone wall was knocked flat to the ground to allow cattle or other farm animals access. Afterwards, the dry-stone wall was built up again, and the animals grazed away within its protected environs.

Sometimes, when the grass was greener on the other side, a brave animal, most often a hungry cow, would bulldoze her way through a stone wall, knocking it flat ahead of her. A full herd, usually five or six cows, followed suit. Most often, this particular field was earmarked as a meadow for winter fodder. The escapees would enjoy a fine feast of sweet and lush grass before being noticed by their owner.

Indeed, they could also knock down a stone wall and break into a neighbour's field, and a harsh quarrel would ensue between the two farmers after cows or bullocks scoffed a colossal section of their grazing field. The threat of a two-pronged pike up the backside of either quarrelling person was a regular occurrence back then. Most times it was an idle threat and they made amends within a few days. But there was always the exception, with a begrudger continuing with the bickering and never speaking to the neighbouring farmer again.

Both Ted and I always took great delight in helping Grandpa to rebuild the stone walls of our fields. Having been built without mortar, they were unstable and often had to be reconstructed. We handed him the smaller stones that were within our lifting power, and he reset the walls to their original shape. Afterwards, the three of us would stand back and admire his creative work.

On occasion, my brother and I would stand on top of the low, mossy stone walls beside our farm to get a better view of our surroundings and decide which field we might wander into next. Neighbouring children would holler at us from afar and we'd scamper from one field to the next, crossing or stumbling over the walls in our hurry to play with them.

The low dry-stone walls at the crossroads parallel to our home provided a place for neighbours to sit and chat on Sunday evenings. Sometimes, a neighbour would bring along a button accordion, or another might bring a fiddle, after which reels and slip jigs were danced by the gathering until the summer sun went down behind the mountains.

Next morning, Nano grumbled, "There was a lot of *rí rá agus ruaille buaille* going on at the crossroads last night." She was the only one who grumbled about such fun and merriment.

It has been a privilege for me to have lived in such simple times, back in rural Ireland of the 1950s. But, more so to have spent my childhood years amongst the speckled-grey, dry-stone walls, which spread far and wide, creating a green patchwork across Gorse Valley. To this day, I still admire dry-stone walls whenever I come across them on my travels, because I know the work that went into constructing and maintaining them.

Drawing in the Hay

The excitement was palpable, and from early June onwards, the air was bursting with anticipation. All the children in our school were aware that, in a few weeks' time, our summer holidays would begin. We were not going to miss the drudgery of school or our teachers.

At last, the day arrived when school was out for the summer, along with the discipline of its establishment. During this time, Ted and I were free to go to the creamery with Grandpa and Neddy every day. We were also free to help Nano make butter, in the old wooden butter churn, by turning the handle again and again, whenever she wished to do so. Best of all, we were free to stay outdoors until the sun disappeared behind the mountains in Gorse Valley.

While we still had some farm chores to do, we had much more time to play. A lengthy daily frolic on the strand, our treasured playground, was always first choice. We spent time with Neddy, haltering him in hope he was in a cooperative mood for some bareback rides around the paddock.

Sometimes, neighbouring friends called by, and we whipped the wheels of bicycles in the haggard with ash sticks. Running wild through green rush-filled fields and scaling low stone walls to see what treasure we might find on the other side was delightful for all.

Ted, though timid-natured in most ways, had a love for climbing trees, which he often did. I always stood by watching while he performed his tree-climbing acrobatics. One summer day, I had a heart-stopping experience when a branch Ted was holding snapped, and he fell to the ground with a huge thud.

The blood rushed to my head and my face burned, as I was sure my much-loved big brother was dead. He lay on the ground, breathless, moaning and groaning as I stroked his bushy red hair.

"Maggie ... get Mum," he said, though I could hardly hear him.

I was glad we were near our home that day, so I didn't have too far to run. When I got near our door, I hollered for Mum, and we were back to Ted at lightning speed. Mum figured he was more winded than seriously hurt, so she sat him up, rubbed his back, and he recovered after a while.

After that day, whenever he attempted to climb a tree, with fear in my heart, I reminded him of what Mum said: "Ted, don't ever, ever climb a tree in your life again."

Sometimes, during these sizzling summer days, we went to the local shop with Nano, and she bought us penny bars or large sumptuous-tasting wafer ice creams. Of course, we visited Mrs O'Brien daily to make sure she was okay, and we did whatever chores needed doing for her.

The much-anticipated time and the excitement of drawing in the hay – Danjoe's hay – arrived. Along with two of his own children, we helped our lovely neighbour to oil the two wheels of his wooden flat-bedded hay cart, known to some as a hay float. He examined its winching system to make sure it worked and checked that its wooden shafts were in good working order too. His pride and joy, Molly, was then yoked up to it.

On our journey to the hayfield, which was quite a distance along the road from his farm, four or five neighbouring children joined us. They jumped onboard the hay cart, all eager to partake in the fun of drawing in the hay.

Sitting up front beside Danjoe, my legs dangling from the cart, it was pure joy to watch Molly, his muscular chestnut-brown horse, pull us along. Her head bobbed up and down, her mane windblown with the momentum of her movement. The many brass buckles of her harness jingled and the clippety-clop of her hooves hitting the road was music to my ears.

Once we reached the hayfield, Molly, under her owner's guidance, backed up to the nearest wynd of hay. The hay cart was positioned at a slant, with the high side of it at Molly's rear and the lowest side just touching the bottom of the wynd. With thick ropes wound around the full circle of it, Danjoe, with the help of a bigger boy, began winching it up at a slow rate onto the cart, the winch creaking under the strain of pulling the heavy eight-foot-high haystack.

Disaster struck when the winch rope jammed. Danjoe stood back and peered at it. "Bad cess to it, anyway."

Even at my early age, I knew this to be a casual expression of his annoyance.

He scratched his head as he examined the situation, then gave it a tug this way and that, but it still wouldn't work. With nothing else for it, he ran to the nearest farmyard and borrowed some tools from the farmer, who he knew well. Once back in the hayfield, and with the help of the borrowed tools, he had the winch mechanism fixed in no time and began loading the haystack again.

"All onboard," he shouted when he finished loading it.

Our return journey began with Danjoe guiding Molly with the reins up front, grinning from ear to ear, delighted to be accompanied by six or seven giggling children. A few of us sat on the cart, at the rear end of the haystack, as this was the best travelling position. We all wore T-shirts and shorts in summertime, and our bare legs, which dangled from the cart, were sun-kissed from the glowing orb above. The sweet and somewhat dusty smell of hay wafted from the haystack, and sometimes a warm breeze tossed hayseed from it through our hair. To add to our merriment, the rear of the cart was low to the road and we could jump on and off it, giggling and laughing each time.

Once we arrived at our local shop – Bob's shop – Danjoe pulled on Molly's reins. "Whoa, now, girl, whoa."

This was a command she knew well and stopped on the spot. We all jumped off the hay cart and our wonderful neighbour treated us to large wafer ice-creams, which we scoffed in no time.

We continued our journey, and when we arrived at the farmyard, a squeal of delight rang out as all passengers jumped off the cart. Danjoe wasted no time in unloading the haystack, then gave Molly a full bucket of water to drink. Afterwards, she chewed hay from an old hessian sack, which he tied over her head with a piece of rope knotted at both ends.

Just then, Ada appeared at the kitchen door. "Come, come inside, everyone."

She had buttery soda bread she'd baked earlier, with lashings of Golden Syrup, waiting for us on the table to feast on. Along with this, she had lemonade ready for us to drink and a big mug of tea for her husband.

To our joy, this journey of drawing in the hay was repeated a few times each day, until the last haystack was brought in from the field. On this day, and once Molly was fed, watered, and safely in her paddock, fun and laughter erupted around Danjoe's house. He played sweet tunes on his old Horner button accordion, and all of us children danced around the big wooden kitchen table, as if there was not tomorrow.

Most times during the summer months, hay carts were left in the backyards of the neighbourhood in a tipped-back position, their shafts, held in place with a length of wood, pointing skywards until they were needed again. They made amazing slides for Ted and me, and our neighbouring friends. We climbed up to the top and hurtled down the wooden floor, and it was not unusual to see a gaping hole in someone's pants when their play became too exuberant.

The excitement of having school holidays continued, as there was always another neighbour who had hay to bring in, and the children of the area were more than willing to help. Not forgetting our own hay that needed to be drawn in from the field, situated by the water edge and the tidal waves of the Atlantic Ocean needed close observation for this work to take place.

Danjoe had a heart of gold and had all the time in the world for children.

Nano always said, "Patience and kindness are a gift from above."

And I forever remember that our neighbour had been blessed with an abundance of both.

Maternal Grandmother

While Ted and I lived with Nano, our paternal grandmother, who we loved, we also loved Margaret, our maternal grandmother. I am honoured to be named after her, but my name was shortened to Maggie to distinguish us.

Another perfect lady, with a heart of gold, and like most grandmothers back then in rural Ireland, she wore black clothing, in sharp contrast with her silver hair. When out and about, our gran wore the fashion statement of old around her head: a black shawl. It draped down around her shoulders and was warm and cosy, made of thick wool and fringed at the lower end.

She lived a few townlands away from us in a whitewashed two-storey house, with a bottle-green door and matching window frames. Along with her husband Tom, she had three children, which included our mum Kate, Aunt Maureen, and Uncle Bill. But my brother and I scarcely knew our maternal grandfather Tom, as he suffered from severe arthritis and took to his bed. But before all of this happened, I have an abiding memory of him, with greying hair, dressed in black clothing and causing a racket coming down the stairs in his black hobnail boots.

At just four years of age, I clearly recall his funeral day. Our sisters, Ted and I, immaculately dressed by Mum, sat on a long wooden bench in his bedroom upstairs. At that particular time, I was so small and short, my legs couldn't reach the floor and I swung them back and forth in unison. We watched a priest in black robes bless him and say prayers over him while he was still in his bed.

Following on from the prayers, there was lots of hustle and bustle, with people coming and going. In the meantime, I scampered away unnoticed and hid under the bed in Uncle Bill's room, as, somehow, I knew what was about to take place. Maybe I had seen an elderly neighbour being laid out in a large wooden box before. I was petrified of peering in at dead people in coffins and I still am to this day.

When all had quietened down a little, Ted found me, and we ran downstairs to the living room. We peeped out the window just in time to see the horse-drawn hearse take our grandfather away to his final resting place.

Our Nanny Margaret was the kindest lady ever. Children were dear to her heart, and they came from miles around to visit and chat with her. She always gave them buttery soda bread, with lashings of blackberry jam, and lemonade to drink. It was rare for any to go home without her giving them a few pennies to buy sweets in the shop.

While I loved her dearly, she had one habit that irritated me: she snorted snuff. She sniffed a pinch of the stinky stuff from the back of her hand on a regular basis, and it had the most unpleasant acrid smell.

"Why are you sniffing that stuff, Nanny?" I asked.

"My dearest Maggie, it is medicine for my nose."

From that day onwards, I felt sorry for her, having to sniff the foul-smelling stuff daily, and I still have her tiny snuff box, which is moulded together with age, in safe keeping.

I often heard stories of old about elderly ladies who smoked clay pipes. As it wasn't a ladylike thing to do, they hid the pipes is various places: in the hedge in front of their home, in an outhouse, or anywhere out of sight of prying eyes. Thankfully, Nanny was more genteel and didn't smoke a pipe.

She was devout, and I remember, instead of having a picture hanging on the wall over the head of her bed, she had an enormous set of rosary beads. It was slightly smaller than a hula hoop, with large brown wooden beads, and hung on the dull pink wall from three screws. A wooden cross, depicting Jesus, dangled from it. Before we went to sleep at night, we took part in the rosary with her, and she usually recited the full fifteen decades, though on a smaller set of beads. Whether it was our wish or not, she always had blue plastic rosary beads on white cotton string ready for use by Ted and me, at any given moment.

One or two decades were fine, and we participated as much as a child's concentration allowed, but once it got to the fourth and fifth decade, it wasn't unusual to find Ted or me, or maybe both of us, fast asleep in a single bed next to her big bed. While I remember her being a kind grandmother, helping us in every which way and giving us sweet treats, I also remember that our sleep episodes during rosary time did annoy her because she always told us so the next morning.

Her brother Jack and his wife Joan lived close to her, and they had a big family. After the birth of their tenth child, Joan suffered with what Mum in later years explained to me was severe depression. Both Joan and Jack struggled to take care of their children, in particular newborn baby Mike.

Our grandmother came to the rescue and took care of him for months on end. She adored him, as did his first cousins Mum, Aunt Maureen, and Uncle Bill.

After some more time had passed, Nanny and her brother Jack had a deep discussion about the baby and his mother's state of health. Tears trickled down Jack's face, and with trembling lips he explained that his wife was still unwell, and he was finding it difficult to cope with nine children and his daily work with the local council.

Between herself and her brother, they decided there and then that baby Mike would stay with her for the foreseeable future. He was extremely lucky, as he was dearly loved by his foster family. He became part of their family, and they raised him as if he were their own. Bill was the youngest of Mum's siblings and Mike was ten years younger still.

Though he seemed much older and taller than Ted and me back then, we got to know him well during our many visits to Nanny Margaret's house, and sometimes we even stayed in her home overnight. He had a nickname for us: the two little rascals. In hindsight, I am sure we deserved that title, as I remember us playing many tricks on him.

Mum and Nanny told us many stories about Mike's younger days, which we loved to hear. He began school when he was five years old – the same school as his siblings and his first cousins attended. The children of both families went to school in the morning and came home in the evening together. It was a rather unusual situation, as when he was coming home in the evening, he went into his aunt's house along with his cousins, while his siblings continued on to their own home.

When he made his First Holy Communion and his Confirmation, his aunty bought his outfits for these occasions. No matter what stage of life he was at, his adopted family took immense pleasure in caring for his every need, although they always made sure he was known to all and sundry by his family name of Sullivan – Mike Sullivan.

On finishing primary school, he stayed for a number of years helping Uncle Bill on the farm. By that time, he was well used to farm work and could gather sheep from the mountainside, milk cows, or take care of any situation the same as Bill. He also helped his aunt around the house, bringing in a basket of turf for the fire or going on errands for her.

When he was nineteen years old and now a giant of a man, with piercing blue eyes and a head of black curly hair, he had no option but to emigrate, like Aunt Maureen and many relatives did before him, as local prospects for employment were non-existent. He went to America and his adoptive family and indeed Ted and I, were incredibly sad when he left.

They, nor his biological family, ever heard from him again and were truly heartbroken. Aunt Maureen found out through the grapevine that he went on to build a new life for himself, got married and had a family of his own – two boys.

While I knew Mike was a gentle soul, it was hard to understand why he made no attempt to communicate or visit his relatives in Ireland. Maybe it was because he found it difficult being away from his culture and traditions and felt he couldn't return. He could have resented the fact that he hadn't been brought up by his mother and father along with his siblings, or there could have been some other reason we were never aware of.

Our gran hoped from day to day that her postman would bring a letter to her from her nephew. It never happened, not up to the day she went to her eternal reward. Mum and Uncle Bill missed him dearly, too, and they often recalled how our grandmother yearned to see him again.

As I grew into adulthood and realised the impact his absence had on relatives, particularly so on Mum, I wished that my second cousin would appear from somewhere out of the blue.

Stranded by the Tide

The laborious process of haymaking on our farm began each year in late spring when Pop and Grandpa spread farmyard manure on our hayfield. They loaded the manure up onto Blackie's cart, and with Grandpa guiding her, she drew it to the field where they used four-prong pitchforks to spread the manure out so it evenly covered the area.

On an early July morning, when they were sure the summer sun was going to oblige and stay for a while, they went to the lean-to shed. They took the mowing machine by its wooden shafts and eased it from where it had sheltered throughout the long winter and spring.

Our sickle-bar mower was mainly red in colour – a simple and solid machine with yellow steel-lugged wheels. At the back, it had a bright red cast-iron seat where Pop sat up high, guiding the horses. The cutting of the grass was done by a long bar of steel fingers, with guard plates and a row of triangular blades or knives riveted to it. Power was transmitted from its heavy wheels through gears, a crank, and a connecting rod to the sickle bar.

I can still remember that morning how Grandpa prepared the mower for the task ahead by greasing any moving parts. Following that, he sat on an old wooden box and laid the long bar across his knee. He took his edging stone, which had a wooden handle, and with amazing skill and pride he edged all the blade ends until they shone bright and were razor sharp. Every now and then, he dipped his sharpening stone in a bucket of water to clean off the waste material.

With the mower ready for operation, Pop tackled Bobby and Molly, Danjoe's horse, to it the next morning and headed down the grassy boreen to our meadow field. This particular field was not part of our main farm holding. It was situated close to the water's edge, about a half mile along the strand and surrounded by a dry-stone wall.

My big brother and I once stood on that same wall, and from this vantage point could view a far-off land across the wide expanse of glistening ocean.

"That is America, where Aunt Maureen lives," Ted said.

I put my hands up to my eyes and made pretend binoculars with my index fingers and thumbs, scanning the horizon in the distance. "Oh, yes, yes, it is, Ted."

"Hello, Aunt Maureen," we shouted in unison across the miles, in the hope that she could hear us.

Pop and the pair of horses spent a long sweltering day going around and around the field cutting the grass into swathes with the mower. The whine of the machine could be heard a good distance away and was evidence of busy hay-making.

Grandpa went to oversee the progress they were making during the day and brought food for Pop to eat. When the need arose, Molly and Bobby had ample juicy mouthfuls of freshly cut grass to munch, and buckets of water to drink from a well in one corner of the field.

In the late evening, they returned home, having cut the entire field of grass. Grandpa brought Bobby to the grazing paddock and Danjoe came by and collected Molly. Pop dragged himself to the kitchen table for a cup of tea, exhausted but grateful that the grass in our meadow field had been cut.

When a few days of bright sunshine had passed, the grass was changing from green to a golden colour as it matured into hay. The next step was to turn it, and this process needed all hands-on deck. Grandpa yoked Blackie to her cart, and we all jumped onboard, Grandpa, our sisters, Ted and me, with Sally accompanying us up front as always. Grandpa had already loaded up our haymaking implements, two-prong pitchforks and rakes. We headed down the boreen and across the strand, with Pop riding Bobby, leading the way.

We began our day's work, and to get the grass dry enough for stacking, our team of workers had to toss and turn it umpteen times with pitchforks, lifting and aerating it. While this was arduous work, especially for us children, the warm summer sun on our backs made it bearable.

"Ouch, ouch," I shouted, and hopped a little and then some more. My jaw dropped when I looked down and noticed blood oozing from my foot. I had just impaled it through my sandal with one of the prongs of my hay pike. Grandpa dipped my foot in the nearby salty seawater until he was sure it had been cleansed of any impending infection, then wrapped it in a handkerchief and our work continued. In farming life back then, whether you were sick or in my case having a sore foot, no notice was taken beyond basic care, and you just continued doing whatever chore you had begun.

Later, it was delightful to see Mum arrive with our lunch, a shiny sweet gallon of hot tea and a never-ending supply of buttery bread with jam from her wicker basket. Tea from a sweet gallon, which we got from our local shop, whilst smelling the sweet aroma of the hay, was the best tasting tea ever. Mum served it in white enamel mugs with a blue rim. Our amazing mum always brought us lunch, as a treat, when we were working in the meadow field. We all sat for a while under the shade of a tree, enjoying the sizzling summer day, having our picnic, chatting and laughing.

Once lunch was finished, Mum returned home and we continued tossing, turning, and saving the hay. On occasion, we saw a rabbit or maybe frogs hopping from the swathes of grass as we worked our way along the field. We had made some great progress and even got some of the hay made into *cockeens* – small stacks.

Grandpa mentioned to Pop that everyone was tired and we had done enough work for one day, and suggested we pack up and go home. But, as usual, Pop was stubborn and paid no heed to Grandpa. We had no choice but to keep working. After a while, Grandpa got annoyed with Pop, so much so, he stuck his hay pike in the ground and insisted that we should go home. I breathed a sigh of relief, delighted that grandpa took charge of the situation, as my foot was hurting.

As we reached the gate of the meadow field, we noticed the tide was coming in. We began making our way along the rocky headland of the strand, but with a strong offshore wind picking up, the tide was coming in faster and faster. Soon Blackie was belly-deep in water and finding it difficult to pull the cart over the rock-strewn headland with the sea swell shaking it. Grandpa was doing his best to guide and steady her, while Ted, our sisters and I clung onto the cart for dear life, with Sally huddled between us.

Meanwhile, Pop was riding Bobby bareback on the steep tide side of us. The sea kept rising and roaring like a wild beast, with a raging swell. Bobby was prancing hither and thither, as he didn't like being in deep water, and we could see that Pop was in a lather of perspiration, in a state of panic, trying to keep Bobby calm alongside us, all the while encouraging Blackie to pull the cart with all her might.

"Come on, Blackie girl, pull," he said. "Pull, Blackie, pull. I know you can do this."

In desperation, Cait, Elizabeth, and Ted looked up to Heaven, praying and asking God to save us.

I was white-knuckled holding onto the cart, trembling with fear and certain we were all going to drown.

After what seemed like an eternity, shocked beyond belief, and dripping wet like drowned rats, we reached a higher place on the strand. Though it was covered with piles of rocks and stones from the tide, Blackie managed to pull her load through it. To everyone's great relief, we reached the safety of the boreen.

Blackie, our strong and resilient pony, was from that day onwards our amazing little hero, and she got an extra helping of oats to eat that evening.

Needless to say, our stranded-by-the-tide story, including Blackie's heroism, was repeated many times afterwards. However, Mum and Nano got a rather toned-down version of our close encounter with being washed out to sea, as they would have been furious with Pop for delaying too long in the meadow field.

Mum noticed that I was limping and couldn't believe that nobody told her when she was in the meadow field earlier about my accident with the hay pike. She bathed my sore foot with hot salted water and put a poultice and bandage on it.

Many, many years later, this horrific day, when we were stranded by the tide, comes back to haunt me, especially if I see rough tidal waters. But I did learn a great lesson that particular day: to be careful when using a hay pike and keep my feet well out of the way of its sharp prongs.

The Banshee

Some Irish legends have been known to say the banshee is the ghost of a woman who was brutally killed. Because of this, her spirit remains to warn Irish families by terrifying screaming and lamenting of an impending death in the family. Her haunting, high-pitched cries aroused terror and dread, and were usually heard in the blackness of night.

Legend has it that she is a ghostly being – an ugly woman dressed in white raggedy clothing, with a hooded cloak that covers most of her fearsome face. She has long, windblown grey hair, long pointed fingernails, and sharp rotten teeth. Her eyes are bloodshot red, thought to be from her constant crying and lamenting.

It was also believed that the banshee would only warn families with certain surnames of an impending death. Surnames beginning with an 'O', and whether this was true or not, any family whose surname came under that umbrella was petrified of this demonic woman. Pop was certain that our surname, O'Caddel, was on her impending-death list, and he told anyone that would listen so.

Stories about the banshee were often told and retold by folk in the rambling houses, where people gathered, shared stories, played card games, gossiped, and sometimes sang and danced. With no television back then, this was their way of passing long dreary winter evenings. My grandparents, for whatever reason, made sure that these scary stories reached my ears, and those of my siblings too.

One such tale related to a man returning in the darkness of night from a visit to a neighbour's house, where they had been playing cards. With the light of his flashlamp, he spied a banshee sitting on the wall of a narrow bridge, brushing her raggedy silver hair.

In the blink of an eye, she disappeared into the night but left her brush behind on the bridge. He picked it up and took it home with him.

Later that night, she came to his bedroom window and asked for her brush. Too petrified to venture close to her, the man grabbed a broom and handed her the hairbrush on the bristle end of it. Thinking the broom was the man's hand, she broke it in two fair halves.

Pop's Aunt Mary, Grandpa's sister, lived four townlands away. She was a kind-hearted and pleasant lady, in her 90th year. Having suffered with arthritis for many years, walking any distance proved difficult for her. As a result of this, she needed assistance with everyday living and grocery shopping. A kind neighbour called by her house daily to help her out.

The distance to our grand-aunt's house was just under three miles, a journey Pop made once a week to make sure she was okay and to check that she had enough food to eat. He undertook this journey in the dark of night, for that was the only time available to him because of his busy life farming during the day and well into late evening. I always knew when he was going to visit Mary because he whistled non-stop for quite a while beforehand – the same happy whistling he did before he visited the local pub on the odd occasion for a pint of porter.

One particular night, Mum packed a bag full of food stuff for Mary, including her regular medication, and I helped her pack it, as I always liked to do.

Pop began the journey to her house on foot, with only a battery-operated flashlamp to light his way in the dark wintery night. His regular mode of transport, his black Prefect car, was out of commission. It had a broken front light, and a replacement wasn't yet available.

With the bag across his back, he had only walked a short distance along the road when he heard strange noises in the distance. As the noises came closer, he began to shiver, as he recognised them as the high-pitched screaming and lamenting of the banshee.

Now, Pop was a man with nerves of steel, but so frightened was he that night hearing her, his heart was thundering, his hands trembling, and his knees shaking. He managed to climb over a low stone wall at the side of the road and, knowing she was following him, for he could still hear her wailing, crept along inside the ditches and hedges for a considerable distance, his heart pounding all the time.

When he realised all was quiet, he sat on a large boulder inside the ditch of a small field to draw his breath. He was still shivering, bedraggled and exhausted after scrambling through many obstacles. His flashlamp cast a faint glimmer through the wind-whipped darkness of the night, and he hoped the battery wouldn't fail. But more so, he worried about his aunt, aware of her fragility at 90 years of age.

His few moments of respite ended rather abruptly, as he could hear the screaming once again. Pop had thought this fearsome wraith had turned her ire on someone else but, as the sound drew closer, he was terrified that it was his aunt's impending death being heralded.

Ashen faced and trembling with fright, he stumbled to his aunt's door. His brown tweed trousers and handknitted jumper were tattered and torn after crawling through so many ditches, and his hands and face were full of cuts and scrapes. At least the satchel containing Mary's food and medicine was made of thick canvas and survived the ordeal.

"What happened, Jimmy," she asked?"

"You will not believe it. I just heard the banshee."

"Sit down, sit down by the fire, and I'll make you a cup of tea."

"Thank you, I will, I'm shivering cold."

As his aunt took her flowery fine bone china cups from the dresser, Pop rubbed his hands together while warming them at the blazing fire. She made him a big pot of tea and served it with fresh buttery buns and homemade blackberry jam. Having expected Pop to call by, for he did so every Tuesday night, our grand aunt, assisted by her lovely neighbour, had baked the currant buns earlier that day.

Pop and Mary chatted for a while sitting by the fire, exchanging the latest news about both of their neighbourhoods. She told him she hadn't been feeling too well for the past few days but reassured him that she was fine. He brought in a basket of turf for her fire and made sure it blazed to heat her living room.

Still shaken and scared, he said goodbye to his aunt and began his journey home.

The next morning, as we all sat at the table, Mum knew Pop was perturbed when he didn't finish eating his breakfast.

"What's wrong, Jimmy? You don't appear to be yourself this morning. And what happened to your face and hands?"

"Ach, I heard the terrifying screaming and lamenting of the banshee, and she got close to me. She even followed me to Aunt Mary's house."

He continued to tell us all about his frightening ordeal and how, still petrified, he began his journey home. His aunt had given him a lend of her flashlamp to light his way and he walked along the side of the road as quiet as a mouse, terrified that the banshee would follow him again. He explained that even the rustling of a tree in the dark chilly night, and the meowing of a cat somewhere along the way, caused his teeth to clatter and gave him body quivers thinking it was her again.

I heard him whisper to Mum that he had a large glass of brandy when he reached the safety of our home to settle his nerves before going to bed.

"Don't let the banshee upset you so much," Mum said. "Keep yourself busy during the day and you'll forget about her."

"Okay, okay, I will try my best."

Having taken Mum's advice, Pop busied himself with farm work that day. Two or three days went by, and sure enough a telegram arrived for him through the local post office, confirming the sad news that a relative of his, who was living in London, had passed away peacefully in his sleep. As sad as it was, he felt relieved that his Aunt Mary hadn't been the target of the banshee from the other night.

Given the slightest opportunity, and for many years afterwards, Pop retold the tale about his close encounter with the banshee, a story forever etched in my mind.

The Banshee

That wail of dread that haunts the air,
All fear the banshee's cry,
A harbinger of death who warns of loved ones set to die,
Her eyes of torment glowing red,
Screams that fill each soul with fright.
What's worse is that one never knows
Who the banshee may call tonight.

- Maggie -

Fair Day

Two crazy bullocks, an eight-mile walk, and a much-anticipated fair day was not for the fainthearted.

I remember one particular fair day rather well, as Pop and Grandpa had to be out of their warm beds at 4am. They made such a racket that morning, waking everyone else in our house. Their task was to herd the cattle to the fair, in a town an eight-mile walk along the road from our farm holding.

A bullock, putting it bluntly, is a male bovine animal that has been castrated and raised for beef. These two were short horn roan yearlings. They had snow-white heads and were bulky, with an abundance of energy.

Pop and Grandpa had anticipated this fair day for a long time, as money was scarce and our family income needed replenishing. Although these two beasts were not our special pets, Ted and I were sorry to see them or any of our animals go. But we did understand why they were being sold.

Mum boiled two large eggs each for Pop and Grandpa that morning, which they ate with plenty of homemade soda bread and big mugs of tea. She knew from the past that fair days are long drawn-out affairs and made sure her menfolk were well fed.

Pop and Grandpa donned their warm clothing and army-green wellington boots. With only the help of an ash stick each, they were ready for the journey of herding the animals to the fair. The sticks were multifunctional, though more for controlling the cattle than to aid walking. Pop commanded the front position, while Grandpa walked behind, swishing his stick to keep them moving.

It is hard to imagine the number of side roads, gates, and boreens along that eight-mile stretch the bullocks could have escaped through. But the herders didn't have a choice and faced their perilous journey with their charges.

Having travelled quite a distance, the bullocks were now away from the familiarity of our farm and the other animals they'd spent their first year of life with, including their mothers. They wandered from one side of the road to the other, stopping here and there and stretching their necks over stonewall ditches, mooing and looking back along the way they'd come. Neither of them understood what was happening, and their ultimate aim was to go back to their herd.

There were many potential escape routes. When they passed low hedges or farmyard walls, they gaped across the top, as if contemplating a leap to freedom. Meanwhile, Pop and Grandpa, dripping with perspiration, were ever vigilant to prevent them getting away. Sometimes, Pop would run well ahead of the beasts and stand guard at the next possible escape route.

In the slanting morning sun, the herding was going reasonably well for a while until they came across a low stone wall. Pop stood guard so the cattle wouldn't jump over it. In his effort to stop them, he took one step backwards too far and toppled over the wall. He disappeared, and Grandpa howled with laughter, as all he could see was Pop's green boots pointing skywards over the wall. Pop grunted, roared, and shouted a stream of expletives from the other side of it, but it only got worse because the animals took advantage of the situation.

The highly agitated beasts jumped the wall and narrowly avoided landing on Pop. With their heads held high and their tails in the air, they galloped to the other end of the rush-strewn field. Their herders feared they were going to jump the next stone wall and onto the strand, at which time there would be no stopping them. Breathless and sweating, with their sticks swishing, they managed to round them up and herd the excited escapees back to the road.

Somewhere along the next part of the journey, Pop and Grandpa breathed a sigh of relief when they came upon another set of herders. The men were also going to the fair, with four similar animals, and they joined forces. It made it easier to herd the cattle as a group, providing support until they reached the fair town. Even though the creatures mingled together, each farmer knew their own from their colour markings.

When they arrived at the town square, many farmers had already gathered, with their animals separated from each other by flailing ash sticks and loud roaring and shouting. It had been raining there earlier in the morning, and mucky, slimy cattle manure was spattered everywhere. The frightened livestock were forced to stand against the walls of the surrounding buildings, mooing skittishly, threatening to escape at any moment. They were not used to such noise and commotion, with people rushing hither and thither. Pop and Grandpa claimed a space for their prized bullocks and waited for the cattle dealers to arrive.

While this was a local fair, it attracted stallholders, who sold religious goods, sewing accessories, Delftware, and much more. It was a day out and about for the community, whether or not they were interested in the buying and selling that took place.

By noon, the five pubs in the town were overflowing. Cattle buyers and sellers, in a celebratory mood, were drinking in little groups outside the pub doors, with some swaying and trying to steady themselves, having indulged in too much alcohol.

Cattle dealers, also known as jobbers, were shrewd operators, with tremendous bargaining skills, and they moved from one fair to the next doing similar trading. Little men with weatherbeaten faces, they had the gift of the gab, and persistence beyond measure. One of their best skills was to catch an unwary farmer and strike a great bargain, for themselves. They operated with cunning, and it was hard to feel sorry for them when, on occasion, they received little in return for their trading efforts.

When the dealers approached Pop, they opened the hostilities by belittling his hefty livestock.

"They're a hungry-looking bunch. You must have run out of grass weeks ago."

Pop had a serious dislike for the dealers but couldn't afford to let his anger show. He managed the would-be buyers by ignoring their insults, only speaking to them when they asked his price. Grandpa stood by, waiting to support Pop when necessary.

"Are you selling?" the dealers asked.

"I might be," Pop replied. "I might be selling both of them together."

"What price are you asking for them?"

This went on, with the dealers continuing to belittle Pop's prized animals. He ignored them and whispered unpleasant words about them to Grandpa. When he stated his price, they came back with a less favourable offer, and Pop ignored them once again. He kept doing this until they raised their offer within bargaining distance of his price.

Soon afterwards, Pop and the dealers spat on the palms of their hands – a signal to show that an agreement was reached – shook hands, and the deal was done. They exchanged cash for the bullocks and parted ways, but not before the dealers received token luck money from Pop.

In the meantime, all family members at home, including Ted and me, managed the daily farm duties. Our thoughts were with Pop and Grandpa and the hardship they had to endure that day. We knew of this hardship from tales of old.

Later that evening, Mum and Ted yoked Blackie to the trap and headed into town to meet up with Pop and Grandpa. They hoped the animals were sold and our menfolk wouldn't have to walk them back home along that eight-mile journey again.

After being assured by Pop and Grandpa that the beasts were indeed sold, Mum and Ted did some grocery shopping and paid a few overdue bills. In the meantime, Pop and Grandpa had a few well-deserved pints of porter, and they all returned home in the trap, pulled by a willing Blackie.

I waited with eagerness for Ted to come home, as I knew that on the return journey, with a couple of pints of porter in their bellies, Pop and Grandpa would be in a talkative mood and be happy to recount the day's exploits. My big brother told me the full story before we went to sleep that night and we roared laughing at Pop's misadventure.

While taking cattle to the fair on foot was challenging and hard work, Pop and Grandpa knew it was a task that had to be done. The money from their sale was needed to keep our meagre family budget afloat – normality for farming communities in rural Ireland in the 1950s.

Where the Fairies Lived

Whitethorn trees grew everywhere in Gorse Valley and could be seen in hedgerows, glens, and on sea cliffs. But to Ted and me, a lone whitethorn tree was something to be feared and avoided at all times.

The cute wooden fairy doors, fairy gardens, woodland fairy trails, and the stories they represent, are delightful in these modern times, but related stories in our childhood were somewhat unpleasant. The wider community of Gorse Valley believed in fairies and were in fear of their power and spells. When neighbours gathered together around their open-hearth fires in the evening, they sometimes shared fairy stories that had been passed down from one generation to the next.

In Irish folklore, the Tuatha de Danan were one of the first tribes to arrive in Ireland, and they were a magical and secretive people. When another warrior tribe, the Milesians, arrived in Ireland, they tried to defeat them, but the brave Tuatha de Danan would not be forced to leave and used their magical powers to shrink themselves and live underground. They travelled underground from one fairy mound or fort to the next, and all mounds were marked by a lone whitethorn tree.

Also, according to Irish Folklore, fairies are mostly portrayed as difficult or sometimes malevolent creatures and, if annoyed, will cause great distress or torment to humans. It was unwise for anyone to interfere with their sacrosanct places of abode – the old ringforts located on mounds. These eerie places had poisonous rounded cap toadstools growing around their forts, which was a sure signal for Ted and me to stay well clear of them. One of the more disturbing aspects of the folklore for us was that fairies have been known to steal children and swap them with changelings.

They could spoil farm crops such as oats or potatoes, and sometimes caused illness or even death to animals. Not under any circumstances would farmers plough up ground near a fairy fort, and housewives would not spread clothes on the bushes near them to dry. Building houses anywhere near their ringforts was a definite no.

On a seaside cliff field, just a little way from our home, a lone whitethorn tree stood – a deciduous tree with spiny branches. It stood proud on a grassy mound, surrounded by a large circle of stones. A ringfort. It was known by our parents and grandparents that this tree marked the underground living quarters of the fairies. My big brother and I knew from the stories they told us in the past that, indeed, the fairies lived there, and we didn't dare go anywhere near this sinister fairy mound. Even the sight of it put fear in my heart.

The fairies, a magical, sometimes angry, and rarely seen folk, are blamed by the inhabitants of Gorse Valley for many things they cannot explain: a failed harvest, a calf dying, or an illness in the family. As a result, they will not, under any circumstances, disturb the fairies or their living area. Most times, they will try to appease them, leaving bread and milk out after sundown for them to feast on. Children snuck by these fairy mounds without even a whisper, to make sure they didn't disturb them.

Grandpa told Ted and me a fairy story about a man he knew who went out and cut a whitethorn tree with his hatchet. He heard a great shout from under the tree, struck it again, and heard another huge scream coming from below. Scared for his life, he scampered home, and it wasn't long before an illness befell him. He took to his bed and was there for a year. Everyone believed it was the fairies who put a spell on him for cutting their whitethorn tree.

Another time, Grandpa told us a story about a farmer in a nearby townland. A threshing machine remained idle in the haggard of his farm for a few days because a part from its threshing mechanism was broken. One night, the silence was shattered by the loud bellowing sound of its engine. He looked out his bedroom window towards the haggard and, to his utter astonishment, saw a group of fairies around the threshing machine. Some were sitting on it, and some were dancing around it to the sound of its engine. While the farmer was flabbergasted that the monstrous machine was working, he did not interfere with the fairies.

"He/She is away with the fairies" was a phrase we often heard back then to describe someone living in a dreamworld and not facing reality.

This probably happened to me umpteen times. When in school, I spent quite an amount of time gazing out that big classroom window, more than likely thinking of Neddy at home in his green pasture, or anything other than my schoolwork.

Miss Hanan would often say, "Please pay attention, Maggie."

I paid attention for a while but then reverted to my dreamworld.

When Ted and I were walking home from the local shop one evening, just before sundown, we had an encounter with the fairies. We were in our own little world, chatting away and eating delicious chocolate bars we had just bought.

Next thing, we heard rustling inside a stone-wall ditch just ahead of us. With our hearts pounding, we were too petrified to pass by, sure it was the fairies dancing. Having been told that the fairies come out when the sun goes down and they like to dance, sing, and have parties around the whitethorn tree, we stood frozen to the spot, wondering what to do.

"Let's go back to the shop, Maggie," Ted whispered.

"Okay, okay, Ted."

He grabbed my hand, we turned on our heels, and headed back towards the shop.

Danjoe came by on his bicycle, and, still shivering with fright, we told him our troubles and where we'd heard the rustling. Along with Danjoe, we walked back to the dreaded place we had heard the rustling. Unnerved, he peeped over the wall but jumped back when an old, grey-bearded nanny goat peered up at him, chewing grassy shrubs.

Danjoe turned to us, trying to contain his laughter. "Ted and Maggie d-don't be scared. Don't be frightened. The rustling you heard was only this old black and white goat. A stray goat eating shrubs."

We breathed a sigh of relief, and even said hello to the old goat before continuing our journey home, accompanied by our lovely neighbour.

To my astonishment, some people believed that the fairies could bring good luck. They believed that if you tied a coloured ribbon or piece of colourful fabric around a whitethorn tree, the fairies would hear your wish, and it would come true. I often had some wishes but they were never so important to inspire me to test this theory out.

Sometimes, drifting off to sleep at night was not on our agenda, and most likely we had exhausted the patience of our tired mum, or Nano. We were warned if we didn't go to sleep soon, the fairies would come and grab us. Petrified that they would take us and switch us for changelings, we closed our eyes and fell asleep in quick time.

Because of the many stories that were in circulation back then, our dread of the fairies wasn't unfounded. A lone whitethorn tree on a mound was to be avoided at all times, as we believed the fairies lived under it. In fact, the sight of a lone whitethorn tree in adult life is still a stark reminder for me of the dreaded fairies and what they could do to you, if they had a mind to.

Nicknames and Surnames

Stories about County Kerry, and in particular Gorse Valley and surrounding areas, would not be complete without mentioning the nicknames and surnames that prevailed within, and which had many distinct aspects and peculiarities.

In the 1950s and beyond, many people in the townland and surrounds had the same forename and surname, and quite a number of the inhabitants were related to each other. It was sometimes difficult to figure out who was who. But all was not lost, as nicknames and other ingenious systems of identification were devised.

My brother and I often discussed the matter and found it difficult to figure out how someone's name was John Bat Dan, but there was a simple explanation. John's surname was Morain, but there were two other Johns living nearby with the same surname. To distinguish him from these two men, he was called John after his father, Bat after his grandfather, and Dan after his great grandfather. And the other two Johns had a similar litany of names: John Joe Tim and John Dinny Pete. This identified all three Johns, and their surnames were only ever used in an official capacity.

There were three Donal Murphys in the townland, and all of a similar age.

"Did you hear about Donal Murphy and his new car?"

"Which Donal Murphy is that? Donal Murphy near the school or Donal Murphy at the crossroads?"

"Neither – Donal Murphy that lives beside the church.

Sometimes, there were two Seáns in a family. The youngest was referred to as Seán Óg – Young Seán – and the other

Seán Mór – Big Seán – who was either the child's father or grandfather.

Luckily, when two pupils in our class in school had the same Christian and surname, our teacher, Miss Hanan, had a simpler way of identifying them. She made sure one sat at the back of the class and the other one sat at the front. Whichever one she needed to speak to, she called out their name while glaring right at them through her thick rimmed spectacles. Not sure how she managed the situation if an additional pupil had the same name.

To make matters even more complicated, another identification system was popular, in the form of a nickname. It involved identifying people by some physical affliction they or their forefathers might have had, or how they dressed, their habits, their trade, or speech patterns – the list goes on. The beholder of the nickname, more often than not, was the last person on earth to be aware of how they were identified by others. But sometimes they were surprised and enlightened by a slip of the tongue.

One particular neighbour was called Johnny Shoemaker. He made leather shoes in his small cobbler shop, and that was a good enough reason to identify him by his trade.

I found it strange that a spotty teenage boy, who lived in a swanky house beside the school, was called Críostóir Rua – Redhaired Christopher. And his sister, a pretty girl with long black hair, was called Bunny, as her top front teeth were prominent.

To add to the hilarity of it all, there were two grey-haired elderly brothers living in thatched cottages close to where we lived, whose wives shared the name Mary. The wife of one of the brothers, Seán, was known as Mary Seán, while the wife of the other brother, Mike, was called Mary Mike.

It was years later when I realised that my older sisters Cait and Elizabeth called me Scrawny Maggie, as I was slight in stature. Mum freaked out a little one day when she overheard them laughing and giggling about how they were addressing me.

"Cait and Elizabeth, if I hear you two calling your sister Scrawny Maggie again, I will kill you both stone dead."

Mum, of course, was never in her wildest dreams going to carry out this threat, but it was enough to scare them, for a while at least.

It wasn't unusual for children in our townland and surrounds, including Ted and me, to be well into adulthood before knowing the real identity of some friends and neighbours.

Surely, and to make identification less complicated, they could have chosen different Christian names when there were three or four families in the same townland who had the same surname. Today, it's different, because we have mass media and an unending supply of children's names being hurled at us on an ongoing basis. This resource wasn't available back then and people went with what they thought would work best.

Yet, this strange means of identifying people with the same name was not meant to demean or insult them. It was just a quick way of picking out a person from a group which might contain two or three individuals with the same name. For people with nicknames, they were mostly identified in this way in a spirit of endearment.

Puck Fair

Puck Fair is one of Kerry's biggest and oldest fairs, dating back over 400 years. It takes place each year in the town of Killorglin from August 10-12th, come hell or high water.

The cavalcade of rainbow-coloured, bow-top, barrel-shaped wagons – the homes of the Irish travelling community – parked up on the side of the road leading to the fair, was evidence that great excitement was afoot. Everything they needed to survive clung to the back of the wagons or was stored in boxes underneath the carriages. They were mostly spirited and large families, with their menfolk having horse trading at the fair uppermost on their minds.

Their umpteen tethered cob horses, white with a mixture of brown and black patches, munched grass from the roadside verges. Though they can have some other colour markings, these cobs were their pride and joy. They were strong and placid, bigger than a pony, with full snowy manes and white hair cascading down their legs.

On the first day of the festival, a wild male mountain goat is crowned King of Puck Fair. He is then hoisted high upon a temporary platform in the middle of the town for all to see and admire, chewing on green cabbage, oblivious to the hustle and bustle below.

My brother and I, on a number of occasions, went to Puck Fair with Grandpa and enjoyed all it had to offer children. It was here that we got on a mechanical merry-go-round horse carousel for the first time in our lives. We also got to go on a dodgem car, which was bumpy, scary, and fun all at the same time. The bumping cars, which is what we knew them by, worked by poles leading from them, which scraped along an electrified grid ceiling and transferred power to them. While the arcing sparks they generated and the smell of ozone they produced made me feel a little nauseous, that did not stop me from accompanying my brother and having a bumpy ride on them. A large rickety wheel in the fairground, full of screaming children, spun around and around, but Grandpa wouldn't allow me or Ted on it, as he feared for our safety.

Another memory I have from the festival is of two circus stilt walkers, dressed in clown uniforms, entertaining us and the large crowd of people who looked on. I gazed up high while they performed their balancing acts and tricks, all the time thinking they were going to come crashing down on top of us all.

There were many street traders selling their wares. Crowds gathered around the stalls, captivated by their amazing sales pitches, and lured into buying something they may have no need for. They pitched their prices high to begin with, then lowered them dramatically, which made those present feel that they were getting a bargain of the year. They sold clothes, shoes, and household cooking utensils of all descriptions. There were sweet and ice cream stalls at the fair, too, which were of particular interest to Ted and me.

Family events, such as bazaars, juggler shows, and Irish dancing were enjoyed by all spectators. Street musicians, playing their instruments to their heart's content, entertained the crowds. Adults had their fortunes told and could also enjoy roulette and many other similar games. There was much hustle and bustle as people moved through the narrow streets from one show to the other.

The Travelling People were a big part of Puck Fair. I loved to watch the women mingle amongst the spectators, wearing thick woollen shawls with flower patterns and fancy fringing at the bottom. The rectangular coverings framed their faces, draped over their shoulders, and underneath they held their babbies to their bosoms, the infants peeking out of the colourful shawls. As they passed, they held their hands out for a few pennies for food to feed their many children.

Cattle were bought and sold on a pitch in one of the town's busiest streets, with palms spat on sealing the deal.

It was amazing to go to the fairground and watch menfolk, mainly from the travelling community, haggle with each other, buying and selling cobs and ponies. Ted and I loved this particular part of Puck Fair, but it enthralled Grandpa, as, of course, equines were his favourite animal of all. It was at this fairground that we met up with Danjoe, on the last visit I remember making to Puck Fair.

"Hey, John, let's go to the pub," Danjoe said to Grandpa.

Off we all went, but we found it difficult to find a public house that wasn't overflowing with people. We walked a while until we found a snug spot, in a thatched pub right on the edge of the town. Danjoe bought a creamy pint of porter for Grandpa and lemonade for himself, Ted, and me.

"Ted, would you like a taste of my pint?" Grandpa asked.

Ted took one sip and, sour-faced, spat it into his cupped hands. "Grandpa, I have no idea how on earth you can drink that horrible stuff."

Townspeople, especially those with business premises, had some misgivings about the fair days. On the one hand, they welcomed the sales of their respective products and services that the fair generated – public houses, restaurants, hardware and drapery shops all did well on these days – but, on the other hand, the fairs turned their town into an almighty mess.

The streets reeked of rotten eggs – the smell the animal dung produced. It splashed on the beautiful painted walls of the buildings and seeped down each street, especially if it was raining. Wellington boots were a must for all to wear, and slipping on the slimy mud of the cobblestoned walkways was hard to avoid. It was a common occurrence for an unsuspecting fairgoer to slip and whack their rear end on the slimy pavement.

Council workers spent day upon day hosing down and cleaning the buildings and the streets of the town when the fair ended.

On the final day of the festival, the goat was dethroned and returned to his mountainside terrain. While my big brother and I didn't like the fact that the poor goat was held captive for three days, high above our heads on a platform, we did enjoy the festivities of the fair.

In recent times, all that has changed, as the goat is treated more humanely. While he will still be crowned King of Puck Fair on its opening day, he will only spend a brief time high up in the stand. He will then leave the wooden platform and make a brief reappearance for his dethroning on the final day of the fair.

Traveller Woman

Mum and Nano would often mention that it must be time for Moll to call by. Whether it was a bright spring morning, in the middle of a scorching summer day, or in the depths of winter, she was sure to appear at our front door.

Wearing a long black tatty dress, with a plaid shawl wrapped around her, greying hair tied back in a tight bun, she'd arrive, and her brash knock was well known to us all. We fondly knew her as Moll because she never disclosed her name. Once she announced her arrival, Ted and I accompanied Mum to the door, as we were curious to see what she had in her basket.

In the meantime, her husband, their cob horse and wagon, with their twelve children, waited patiently across the road from our house. Their eldest, a twelve-year-old daughter, held the baby of the family in her arms, and all siblings, in stair-step age range, peered out the front door of their colourful barrel-shaped home. Their hair and clothes were a little tatty, but they looked joyful and happy. I often wondered if they would like play and have fun with Ted and me, but, for some reason, they never did.

Their bow-top horsedrawn wagon, also known as a vardo, had two big wheels on the rear axle and two smaller wheels on the front one, attached to shafts, all a bright yellow colour. Their canvas-covered living space was mounted on top of the axles, the frame of which was an intricately designed wooden masterpiece, painted a rainbow of colours, and with gold gilding.

Similar to those at Puck Fair, all of their belongings clung to the back of the wagon, with some stored on the underside of the carriage. Cans, pots and pans, galvanised buckets, a bath, bags full of clothes, and much more. All of their drinking and eating vessels were skilfully made of tin so they didn't break during their travels and were also stored in the undercarriage.

"Good day to you, Ma'am," Moll said, when Mum opened the door. She produced her gondola-shaped wicker basket. "Do you want to buy a scissors, Ma'am, or maybe some clothes pegs?"

"No, no, I already have both, so I don't need them."

She shuffled the multitude of items in her basket about. "Maybe you need some sewing needles or thread, Ma'am?

"Okay, I'll take some of them."

And the bargain was agreed, money handed over, but her visit didn't end at that juncture.

"Would you have a drop of milk for the babby, Ma'am?

Mum hurried to the kitchen and gladly brought back some milk in a lemonade bottle.

In the meantime, Moll broke into song on the doorstep and her soothing tones were music to our ears.

"Bless you, Ma'am. Maybe you would have a bit of bread for the childer?"

Mum left the door and arrived back a minute later, with the requested bread.

"The blessings of God on you, Ma'am."

With her black brogue-style boots click clacking, she'd walk a little way down the front path towards the gate. But, after having a quick think about the situation and figuring that Mum was being particularly benevolent, she'd turn on her heels and back she'd come, without Mum even having a chance to close the door.

"Would you have a graineen of sugar for the tae, Ma'am?

"Hmm, okay, okay."

"God spare your health, Ma'am. I'll be off with meself now, and good day to you."

"Bless her," Nano said, once she had gone, "she is just trying to do her best to feed her family."

"Yes, yes, of course she is," Mum replied. "And what a hard life she has."

Sometimes, she even swapped items her tinsmith husband made for food. He made billycans, mugs, wire-handled cooking pots, buckets, and more. All of the items Mum bought from her, whether they were skilfully made by her husband or otherwise, were of the highest quality. Forty years later, Mum still had a breadknife she purchased from our traveller friend.

When she left our house, the dogs of the neighbourhood barked and barked, evidence that she was going around from one neighbour's house to the next. Nano's wish was that, by the time she finished her neighbourhood travels, she had everything she needed for that particular day to feed her large family.

After they finished their daily travels, Moll and her family found a wide and sheltered place on the roadside, where they camped up for the night. Their horse was unharnessed from the wagon and, with a long tether, left to munch grass from the roadside verge. Helped by her eldest daughter, she washed the family clothing in a tub of water. The aromatic bushes of the hedgerows made ideal perches for the colourful laundry, which was dried overnight. They built their campfire, ate the food she had gathered during the day, and sat warming themselves on several types of seating: an upturned galvanised bucket, a round log of wood, or maybe an old wooden half barrel. Their black kettle boiled on the fire for tea and they chatted and sang until it was time to bed down for the night in their cramped vardo.

The community of which Moll and her family were members led a nomadic lifestyle, as that was how many generations before them lived. Back then, they travelled from town to town, offering goods for sale or swapping them and asking for alms, including old clothes for their families. As far as I know, they only asked people who they knew from previous encounters understood their way of life and were benevolent. They were grateful for what offerings they received and lived simply.

Wintertime was particularly hard for the travelling community, as they had no electricity. With frost and snow thick on the ground, the only source of heat they had was from their campfire. They used many layers of old blankets, shawls, and coats, to keep themselves warm while they slept in their vardo home.

They obtained rainwater whenever it fell, which was stored in a steel tank and loaded onto their wagon.

I have fond memories of our nomadic friend calling to our door on a regular basis, but I particularly remember her greying hair brushed back into a tight bun, and her colourful tartan shawl snuggly wrapped around her hefty frame. Her sweet melodic voice was always a joy to hear.

A Parcel from America

One midsummer day, Mum was busy making bread in our kitchen when she heard a knock on the front door. With swift strokes, she wiped the flour off her hands on her apron and opened the door to find Josh our postman standing in front of her. I peeped out to see him smiling from ear to ear, with beads of sweat on his forehead. It was a sweltering day and he had cycled far and wide on his big black postal bike, doing his round. His charcoal-woollen uniform and matching peaked hat, embellished with a shiny harp symbol, no doubt added to his perspiration.

"Good day, Kate," he said, handing Mum some letters. "Oh, and there is a big parcel addressed to you in the post office, but it was too heavy for me to carry on my bicycle.

"No worries, Josh, I will collect it tomorrow. Thank you."

The next morning, and while outdoors doing chores with my brother, I remembered the parcel and ran into the kitchen. "Mum, did you and Pop collect the parcel from the post office?"

"Oh yes, yes, we did, Maggie. Aunt Maureen sent it from San Francisco."

"Where is it? Can we open it."

"Maggie, darling, I am too busy. I don't even have time to bless myself and, anyway, we need to have everyone here to share in the excitement of opening it."

I rolled my eyes to Heaven and scampered out the back door to tell Ted what Mum said.

Later, with all farm chores done, everyone was ready to relax for the evening. With broad smiles, Ted, our sisters and I watched Mum and Pop lift the parcel from under the stairs. It was wrapped in several layers of strong brown paper, with an array of strange stamps, and a neat white address label on it. A United States of America airmail label, with an aeroplane on it, was of particular interest to Ted, as he loved anything to do with planes. The box was tied securely on all sides with rugged twine, and with red sealing wax on all knots.

With the help of a scissors to cut the twine, we unwrapped it on the kitchen table. The beautiful aroma of lavender wafted from the top of the parcel, as a big square of handmade soap, wrapped between a handwritten letter and tied in a bow with purple silk ribbon, appeared. The short letter read:

Dear Kate,

I hope this finds you and your family well. I have been gathering up these clothes and other bits and bobs for the past few months and I sincerely hope that you all like them. I am feeling lonely here in San Francisco and I hope to come to see you all and my beloved Ireland very soon.

Take care, love and best wishes, Maureen x

Aunt Maureen rode away from the mountains, streams, and the family that raised her and went to America at the tender age of nineteen. Mum told us many stories about her and how she left alone, with an old brown suitcase on the carrier of her bike and cycled ten miles to a relative's house, where she stayed overnight.

Before she left, her mother, our kind-hearted grandmother Margaret, sprinkled her with holy water to bless her for her journey. Tearfully, she handed her a small, weathered tin box that contained a few different size rubber patches, sandpaper, rubber solution and a tyre lever – a puncture repair kit – for fear she hit a pothole or uneven bump on the road and got a puncture on the wheel of her bike.

At the break of dawn, the next morning she cycled another five miles to the nearest train station. After she reached the dim smoky station, she left her bike in storage, to be collected by the same relations, whenever they happened to be in the town. Aunt Maureen took a train from there to Cobh, in County Cork, and began a long journey by ship to America. Their first port of call was Liverpool in the United Kingdom, where a huge crowd of people came onboard.

It was in the depths of November and there was a major storm out in the Atlantic Ocean. The captain of the ship had to navigate his way around the worst of it, which meant an extra day was added to an already long and arduous journey.

Several weeks later, Mum received a letter from Aunt Maureen. She said that her journey on her bicycle to the train station was not a pleasant one, as it was raining and cold, but she assured Mum that her train journey to Cobh was reasonably good.

Aunt Maureen said that even though the journey by ship from Cobh to the USA was lengthy, and despite the weather conditions, she met some nice people onboard. Some had brought their old button accordions and flutes with them, and they had merriment, singing, and dancing, managing to keep their spirits high throughout the journey. She mentioned the mouthwatering food they had on the ship and said she had never in her entire life tasted food so good.

She studied hard and became a nurse but, because of her studies and her busy nursing career, she never got an opportunity to meet the man of her dreams, so she remained single. She missed our mum dreadfully, and Mum often shed a tear when she spoke of how far away her sister lived.

The parcel contained two beautiful dresses and matching cardigans for Cait and Elizabeth, which they were delighted with. There was a tweed pair of trousers and a jumper for Ted. Pop got two shirts, one for Sunday and one for work, and Mum received two beautiful flowery blouses. Grandpa got a new black hat, which was neatly packed in a hat box at the bottom of the parcel. To Nano's delight, she received a warm woolly black cardigan, with brass buttons, and three big hanks of knitting wool. My eyes lit up when Mum lifted out a beautiful deep-red woollen coat and matching bonnet. The bonnet had snowy white fur around the front edges and it tied under my chin with strings, which had two matching furry bobbles at the end. I loved that coat and hat set. Elizabeth always helped me to fasten its buttons before she placed the bonnet on my head and I paraded around in it like Little Red Riding Hood.

Aunt Maureen's parcel also contained story books, pencils, rubbers, and little writing pads for us girls. A separate box at the bottom contained five grey toy aeroplanes for Ted. They were diecast military jet aeroplanes, with *US-AF* written in small letters near the tail. His eyes opened wide with sheer delight as he unwrapped his special gift. I was happy for my brother, who deserved this unique gift from Aunt Maureen, as he had a heart of gold. My kind big brother – my idol.

When the excitement of opening the parcel died down, we were all in agreement that Aunt Maureen was so generous to send us this parcel all the way from the United States of America. It was also a reminder that people living in America had a better standard of living than we had in our modest homestead in Gorse Valley, in County Kerry.

Mum wrote a long letter of thanks to Aunt Maureen for the amazing gifts she sent us, and she also told her all the local news. Ted wrote a special little note of thanks for his aeroplanes, and Cait wrote another note of thanks from us girls. Mum enclosed them all in one envelope, addressed it, and posted it the next day.

Some years later, Ted, our sisters and I often joined Mum

in singing a song about San Francisco. Mum's emotional rendition of the song was an indication that she missed her only sister, and she was forever in her thoughts. She was always on cloud nine when Josh arrived with a letter for her from Aunt Maureen, and a parcel from her was the icing on the cake – not just for Mum but for us children, always anticipating the goodies inside.

Threshing Time

Summer was drawing to a close, the autumn wind winnowed its way through the golden oat fields, and the days were getting shorter. It was time for the threshing of the oats – along with the hay, it sustained most of our farm animals through winter, with them being housed indoors and it also provided straw for their bedding.

I can clearly recall one springtime, when Pop and Grandpa, along with Bobby and Danjoe's horse Molly, spent many days in one of our fields preparing it for sowing the oats. They ploughed and harrowed the chosen plot of land, sowed oat seeds in it and they rolled it again to help cover the seeds, to make sure they were pressed into the earth and left to germinate.

Shortly afterwards, my brother and I took great delight in helping Grandpa to place a scarecrow in the centre of the field, to scare away the scavenging crows and prevent them from eating the planted seeds.

Grandpa joined two big pieces of wood together with nails to make a cross-shape frame to hold up the scarecrow. Ted and I made a round stuffed head for him with a piece of hessian sack and decorated it with eyes, a nose and a mouth. We dressed him with an old plaid shirt, gave him bristling straw hair and placed a tatty flat cap on his head. We named our new creation Roddy and for the most part, he did scare away the crows. My brother and I often stopped by the field and, said hello to him."

One particular day we visited Roddy, where he stood alone in the middle of the big field of golden oats. His arms were wide and threatening, but I thought he looked extremely lonely.

"Why are you so sad, Maggie?" Ted asked?

"I'm sad because I feel so sorry for poor Roddy, because he has no company."

Ted thought for a second. "I know, I know what we'll do, Maggie. We'll make him a wife."

We scampered back home and made her from wood, hessian sacking and straw, in a similar way that we helped Grandpa to make Roddy. We grabbed an old skirt and a tattered blouse that Mum didn't wear anymore and Nano gave us a flowery scarf for her head.

We were back in the field in no time – we plonked her up beside Roddy. With his new wife Florence at his side, he stood proudly, and they both looked joyful and happy together.

Many months later in autumn the threshing began, but before it did many examinations of the oat crop took place. I know these thoughts ran through Pop's mind as he stood in the golden field, rubbing and feeling an ear of oats between his thumb and fingers: *Is it ready for harvesting? Is it dry enough? Will it rain tomorrow?*

The possibility that it might rain the next day always played havoc with the best laid plans of farmers. They had a broad knowledge of weather systems back then, handed down to them from one generation to the next. If the mountains seemed closer than usual, rain was on the way. Crows flying low indicated a storm. Red sky at night was farmers' delight, meaning the next day the sun would split the trees.

Once a sunny day was guaranteed, Pop and Grandpa cut the oats and when it was bone dry they brought it back from the field to our farm in a cart, pulled by Bobby. Soon afterwards, the threshing was done by a big farming contractor from a nearby town.

When the dusty pink-and-red threshing machine arrived in our yard, there was great excitement amongst everyone, especially Ted and me. Our neighbours arrived to help – it was necessary to have a number of hefty men to keep the huge machine operating from early morning to late at night. They didn't have to be asked to come, as it was a given that the men of our house would return the favour when it came to the threshing of their oats.

'*Meitheal*' is an Irish word for work team or gang. It is still practised in rural Ireland to this day – a co-operative – where groups of neighbours help each other with farm work such as harvesting. Neighbours who give their time working for others are helped in turn with their seasonal work. It builds resilient communities who thrive together and make life easier for all concerned.

The enormous engine of the threshing machine – powered by a tractor, with wide black pulley belts of many sizes – started up. Ear defenders, which weren't even a thought in anyone's head, should have been worn. The high-pitched noise from that machine would wake the dead as it cut its way through the processing of the oats. It's no exaggeration to say the bellow from its powerful engine could be heard from several miles away. No wonder Grandpa was hard of hearing.

I clearly recall it as being a wonderful time of camaraderie between neighbours. All of the men, with sleeves rolled up and pitchforks in hand, chose whatever work they preferred to do for the threshing of the oats. Two men pitched the sheaves high up to the top of the thresher, and from there two more shifted them down a big chute. Here, the process of threshing began. New straw was spurted out at one end, and oats filled hessian sacks at the other end, with the waste chaff coming out underneath.

When those men got tired, others would row in instead of them. Their foreheads dripped with sweat, but this did not deter them. They worked until every sheaf of oats was loaded onto that monstrous machine. It was a jovial and spirited time when porter was drunk by the barrel and lemonade was plentiful for us children.

Although the two of us thought of the monstrous thresher as a magical machine, we had to heed several warnings from the adults.

"Ted and Maggie, stand back. You two could get sucked in by those enormous pulleys." Or: "Ted and Maggie, stand back, don't put your hands near those pulleys."

One time, Ted grabbed a pitchfork and tried to help the men pitch the sheaves, but all he did was get in their way, as he couldn't keep pace with them. On noticing Pop glaring at him, I grabbed my brother's hand and pulled him out of harm's way.

Mum and Nano worked hard during threshing time, too, cooking bacon, cabbage, and potatoes for one o'clock dinner for about eight men. And, again, at six that evening, they provided an enormous supper for the workers.

The next day, the thresher would arrive on the farm of one of the members of the work team, and before he went home from our house that evening, Pop and Grandpa assured him that they would be there to help.

Our Potato Crop

It was time to dig up our potato crop. Before we planted them in spring, Nano had cut mounds of potatoes in two, which we knew as *sceallàns* or seed potatoes. She made sure that each half of the cut potato had an eye for sprouts to grow, to make sure several floury potatoes grew from it. This procedure was slow and mundane and involved great skill, turning and carefully examining each potato. Nano was the only one with this expertise in our family, and indeed she gave her time freely to do this work for some neighbours too.

Sowing seed potatoes was challenging work, even for supple children like Ted, our sisters and me, but at least the sunny spring weather helped. Nano was never expected to do this work, but the rest of our family spent two days in the field – with wellington boots on our feet, buckets full of seeds in our hands, and backs bent low as we strode along carefully planting each one in the drills or ridges. The loose earthy ground had already been prepared, similar to the preparation of the oat field and ploughed into drills by Pop, Grandpa and their equine team Bobby and Danjoe's horse Molly.

I have fond memories of both horses, who were nearly identical chestnut brown gentle giants, pulling that plough with their heads bobbing up and down and their long manes blowing in the wind, though their white fetlocks were grubby and dirty from the freshly ploughed earth.

The sowing of the seed potatoes was going well, but by the evening time all workers were getting tired and some of us were fed up and just wanted to go home. Ted thought of an ingenious idea to speed up the process. Instead of planting one seed potato at a time, which was the natural order of things, he decided he would plant several in the same spot and cover them up quickly for fear anyone would notice.

"Why are you sowing the seeds like that, Ted?" I whispered.

"You see, Maggie, I just want to get rid of as many seeds as possible in one go. Then we will finish earlier and be able to go home."

"Ted, if Pop sees what you are doing, he will absolutely hit the roof."

But, undaunted he continued and luckily Pop didn't see his method of planting the seeds.

Several months afterwards at the latter end of Autumn, when the potatoes needed to be harvested, the same wonderful team of horses were used again by Pop and Grandpa and the potato crop was ploughed up in no time. That's when the challenging work began again. Donned in rubber boots and buckets ready, our work crew began filling one potato sack after the other.

Once more, we were bent low for many hours gathering up the potatoes with our bare hands, and we had to root deep through the stony clay to find a handful of them.

Pop noticed that there were clumps of potatoes in certain spots and he scratched his head wondering why it had happened. That particular day, Ted looked at me, the colour was draining from his face and I bit my lip to prevent an outburst of laughter, as I knew well the reason for the mysterious cluster of potatoes.

I have vivid memories of Cait getting annoyed with the picking of the potatoes, as it appeared she had lost her patience for the task. She'd grab a full but withered stalk of potatoes and shake it to death until all the potatoes fell to the ground. Red faced, she'd pick them up and fling them into her bucket. Elizabeth never complained, she just did what was expected of her.

We worked late into the evenings and the frosty air numbed our fingertips. I often wondered why Pop left picking our potatoes until late into autumn, as our neighbours always had their crop dug up and pitted well before the frosty evenings. Grandpa reminded him several times,

"Jimmy, let's pick the potatoes, it's getting late in the year and the frosty evenings are closing in." But Pop ignored his prompts and it was hard to fathom what went on in that man's head.

When the picking work was eventually done, the sacks of potatoes were carried to the headland of our field. With spades, Pop and Grandpa dug an enormous square patch into the ground, about nine inches deep, and emptied the potatoes into it, in one big heap. This heap was called a pit of spuds or potatoes. The pit was covered with multiple layers of oaten straw and topped off with mounds of clay to protect them through the winter. A full sack of potatoes was brought home from the pit as needed, on Neddy's back.

While I knew that it was work that needed to be done, so that we would have potatoes for dinner for many months afterwards, those bitter cold evenings in that potato field will forever be etched in my memory.

Halloween

Before the harsh weather arrived, we celebrated Halloween on the last day of October. In the simplest terms, it is a festival celebrating the changing of the seasons from light to dark – summer to winter. As these two periods cross over, the dead supposedly return to the mortal world and people dress up in costumes resembling witches, skeletons, and vampires, and light bonfires to ward off evil spirits.

I don't remember Ted, our sisters or me dressing up in scary costumes or going around from house-to-house trick or treating. We had a more family focused celebration of Halloween.

Mum helped us to suspend an apple from the ceiling with twine, and we took turns taking bites or chunks out of it. The game was called 'snap apple'. I recall it being a difficult manoeuvre, as our hands were tied behind our backs and the apple swung around and around. We sometimes got lightheaded and dizzy trying to bite the apple. I remember one time, Elizabeth got so woozy she plopped on the floor and hurt her wrist. One thing is for sure, the kitchen was filled with laughter during these Halloween games.

When we got tired of playing that game, we played a different one, where we filled a basin full of water and put several apples into it. We took turns dunking our heads in it to snap a piece out of the apple. It was difficult to bite the apple, as the basin was placed on the concrete floor and the apples bobbed up and down in the liquid.

When it was my turn, I dunked my head in the water and instead of biting the apple, I took a ginormous gulp of liquid into my mouth and up my nose. I coughed and gagged on the water trying to catch my breath and spurted it all over Ted. I was a mess with watery slimy stuff all over my face and Ted was drenched. We looked at each other and howled with laughter.

The rosy, red apples were picked fresh from our orchard, they were delicious and the first person to bite a decent chunk out of the apple was the winner and was allowed to eat the entire apple.

During the late evening, our family feasted on barmbrack – a cake filled with delicious raisins and sultanas and we scoffed it along with tea. We burst with laughter and excitement trying to find the ring or coin wrapped in baking paper in the cake slices. The belief was that the finder of the ring would marry within a year, and if you found the coin, wealth would come your way. I don't ever remember much wealth coming our way, and Cait, the finder of the golden ring declared that she was not going to marry the boy who lived a townland away.

As Halloween evening was drawing to a close, Nano went into overdrive again with her Mass and prayers. She reminded our sisters, Ted and me to go to bed early, as we needed to be in church the next morning to attend Mass for All Saints Day, the first day of November – we duly did as she requested and our entire family attended Mass the next day. It was a holy day of obligation, and we remembered the martyrs who had given their lives in the name of God.

Come the evening of that particular day, Nano gave us the very same reminder again, at which time she totally confused me.

"Why on earth do we have to go to Mass again tomorrow?" I whispered to Ted, back then.

"I don't know, Maggie, but maybe if we don't go, we will commit a sin and end up in purgatory. Surely you remember those stories Nano told us about it. It's a place of punishment you go to if you sin, and you won't get out a there and end up in Heaven until you are sorry for them."

"Well, I'm not going to that place, Ted, so I better do what Nano suggested."

Off we went to Mass again the next morning the second day of November, to appease the devout Nano and not end up in a place we had no wish to visit. This second day of prayer was to remember family members, deceased relatives and neighbours, who had the misfortune to end up in purgatory.

At this time of year, activity on our farm was slowing down, as the long dark evenings of winter had closed in. Little or no work took place in the fields and the animals were warm and snug in their sheds.

Even though we loved farming life, my brother and I were delighted that the most arduous and mundane chores of the year had come to an end. We had more time to play and figure out what mischief was next on our agenda.

However, on looking back, being so involved in farm work played an important part in shaping us young ones into the adults of today. Through our childhood years, we were often reminded by adult family members that hard work never killed anyone.

A Gaggle of Geese

Without exception, Ada had an extraordinary welcome for all children in our neighbourhood and the wider locality. Children would come from far and near to visit her, including Ted and me. I loved her buttery soda bread, laden with golden syrup, which was scrumptious.

Regardless of Ada's warm welcome, sometimes visiting her house could be rather perilous, for she always had a gaggle of geese or two being fattened for Christmas time.

An Embden breed, Ada's geese had snowy white plumage, with orange beaks, and icy-blue eyes. They originated from the northwestern German town of Embden, hence their name. These geese strutted around, taking up a sizeable area of the narrow roadway near Ada's homestead, as if it was their domain. The road was quiet in the 1950s, with only a handful of cars passing by in any one day. Ready to attack, all ten to twelve of them observed everyone who came and went.

When attempting to visit Ada and get past her flock of geese, we would throw a pebble or two in the opposite direction of the one we were heading in, with the intention of getting the geese to turn their heads. If they were distracted, our hope was to sneak by unnoticed. But they were too clever. Those nasty birds would fly at us, flapping their wings with anger in their eyes. Petrified that they would leave us sightless, we would turn and run like terrified hares.

Sometimes, there was a possibility that, later in the day, we could continue our journey unhampered. Ada, assisted by Shep, her black and white collie dog, with his flawless rounding-up skills, made sure those large white birds were contained in the haggard at the back of their farmhouse. The threshing of crops took place there in early autumn and the geese had an abundance of food, fattening themselves on the fallen oat grains. We were then free to visit Ada's house without the fear of those birds in our hearts.

Once indoors and in Ada's kitchen, we sat at her big wooden table. She gave us buttery homemade bread, with golden syrup, or, on other occasions, lemonade and biscuits. She told us stories and sang songs and rhymes for us.

Accompanied by one or two of her own children, the two of us would often do some light chores for her, such as bringing in the eggs from the henhouse or fetching water from the well. Sometimes, we made a mash of cold tea, potatoes, bread, and any leftovers from their earlier family dinner, and fed Shep with it for her.

The flock of geese slept in a stone-built shed at night, to make sure Mr Fox did not come prowling and feast on one or two of them. We visited Ada early one particular morning and she asked Ted and me to let the geese out of their shed. We opened the door and ran for our lives as the geese exploded out of their quarters. They chased us with flapping wings, then gathered in a group and appeared to laugh at our near-death experience. I hoped against hope that Ada would never again ask us to do this particular chore.

When it was time for us to go home, she gave us a little bag of sweets and asked us to call by again soon.

When Christmas was approaching one year, I was in their kitchen and I overheard Danjoe and Ada discussing the geese. I remember that Ada was sad that she would never hear the honking or hissing of her geese again, or at least until the next batch hatched later in the next year. She knew the time was drawing closer and the demise of her large white birds was imminent. To her, they were pets she'd hand reared since the day they were hatched out.

"Why are you so sad, Ada?" Danjoe asked her.

Tears trickled down her face. "I don't … I don't want to do this!"

"I totally understand your anxiety about the passing of your geese, Ada, but we have no other choice. We need a fatted goose for Christmas dinner, and we need the money from the sale of the rest of the flock to tide us over into the new year."

Troops of neighbours got together – a good mixture of both men and women – and a certain barn was sourced as the location for the demise of Ada's geese, and the geese belonging to many other women in the locality. When the horrendous process of killing and scalding the geese had finished, the plucking of feathers and down began in earnest. The covering that insulated the geese in the past months flew here, there, and everywhere. By the time the neighbourly troop had finished plucking all the geese, the floor of the barn looked like a snowstorm had hit it. Turkeys were reared in the same way and, unfortunately for them, their demise came about soon after the geese.

Ada once told Mum a story about a woman she knew, whose name was Hanna. Similar to Ada, she always raised a flock of turkeys for the Christmas season. However, she didn't have a turkey cock of her own, as a fox had feasted on it.

Once the time arrived when her turkey hen became broody, she dutifully took her to a near neighbour's farm to make her acquaintance with their turkey cock. She placed her turkey hen in a hessian sack, with her head peeking out, and put her on the carrier of her bicycle, tying the sack with string so her prized turkey didn't fall off on the journey. They soon arrived at the neighbour's farm, where the turkey cock gobbled and strutted around, with his waffle blazing red and his wings and tail fanned out. The hen was introduced to him, at which time he began to strut and dance around her. They made their acquaintance and, later that day, Hanna took her turkey hen home again.

The hen found a safe and quiet place to nest and, fourteen days later laid ten eggs in the same number of days. After sitting on and incubating her eggs for twenty-eight days, her fluffy turkey chicks emerged one by one.

Once the plucking of the geese for Christmas was complete, the white feather and down was transported to the nearest big town, where it was processed into filling for tick pillows and mattresses.

Our actual pillows were made of goose feather and down, encased in tight-woven grey and white-striped cotton ticking. Even so, I will never forget how those horrendous feather quills were sure to poke through and stab me in the face as I tried to sleep. Our mattresses, on the other hand, were made of the finest horsehair and were the height of comfort.

When the plucking marathon was complete, it was then up to all and sundry to take their plucked goose home for Christmas dinner. The geese that were left over were sent to a local market and sold.

In our household, the plucked goose that Mum bought from Ada was hung on the back door, with its feet tied together with brown string and long neck hanging below. Its wings were still in-flight mode, which was rather perturbing. Ted and I wished for Christmas day to hurry up and arrive, as we awaited the small gifts that Santa Claus was going to bring us. But, more importantly, we wished, with all our might, that this particular day was actually here, as the sight of this bereft-of-life large bird hanging on our back door scared the living daylights out of us. And having to pass it on our way in and out several times a day only added to our trepidation.

Dead or alive, Ada's geese caused us more worry than we cared for. But even though our regular visits to Ada were an ongoing struggle, we never let a gaggle of geese deter us, especially when the visit included her gorgeous buttery soda bread and golden syrup.

A Bed of Straw

On a bitter cold December evening, my brother and I were peeping out our parlour window, watching a friendly robin redbreast twitter from branch to branch on the old oak tree, which stood high and proud to one side of our back yard. The gale-force winds of autumn had stripped it of its leaves, and on this winter's evening, only a mass of icicle spikes hung from its branches. Undaunted by the ice, the little robin pecked and pecked away, desperate to find a morsel of food.

Next minute, we heard a faint knock on our back door. We ran to the kitchen to alert Mum. When she opened it, there stood a light-framed little man. His face was weather beaten, his grey beard overgrown, and he wore tattered clothes, with an old hat turned sideways on his head that didn't cover his long scraggy hair.

On noticing the sadness on our faces at the sight of this poor man, Mum put her arms around us. "Ted and Maggie don't be sad. That is Paudeen, the journey man."

Once indoors, and after warming his numb hands on our open-hearth fire, he offloaded his wee satchel, which contained all his worldly possessions, and sat by our wooden kitchen table. Mum boiled two eggs for him, and within a short while he devoured them with a big mug of tea and homemade bread. Having rested for a while, he moved away from the table, leaned back on the chair and stretched out his legs. We could see that he'd travelled many miles in the past few days, as his black boots were the worst for wear.

"You could do with another pair of boots, Paudeen," Mum said.

"No, not at all, these boots are fine, Ma'am."

Mum had it in her mind to offer him an old pair of black boots belonging to Grandpa, that still had a bit of wear left in them. It was lucky that Paudeen refused her offer, for if Grandpa knew Mum had given away his footwear, he would not have been too pleased.

Mum later told us that Paudeen was a free-spirited man, and a gifted mouth-organ player, who sang, skipped, and jumped along the roadway while going from one town to the next. He had no fixed abode – a traveller on the road to nowhere. Most times, he slept in an outhouse or barn and would only stay one night in any particular place. A quirky little man, who had no regular occupation, though he was no beggarman, he was always willing to do odd jobs in return for the alms and shelter he received. As he travelled to each town, he always had a particular refuge in mind, with people he felt at ease staying with, who had compassion and empathy with his way of life and who were kind-hearted.

A gifted storyteller, too, Paudeen told us some stories of his travels – whether they were true or not was anyone's guess. One particular story he told was about an acquaintance of his, Johnnyboy, who lived a few towns away and owned a black and white goat named Jacinta. She was as old as the hills, and he tried to sell her on many occasions but always failed to do so.

Determined to sell Jacinta and have a few bob in his pocket, Johnnyboy put a tether around her neck. He took her to a local fair and sat on a wooden bench, with his prized goat in front of him for all to see.

He observed all those who shuffled about the fair, where a wide variety of animals were being bought and sold that day. It was obvious to him that the black stuff – alcohol – was plentiful, being gulped down by men acting like young

175

children who hadn't seen a bottle of milk for a week. Being rather wise, he knew there was a great likelihood he could meet an unsuspecting buyer who had consumed too much of the hard stuff.

Johnnyboy waited his chance with patience, and after a while a man staggered towards him and Jacinta. He sat on the wooden bench beside them and, after they exchanged a few words about the weather, asked him, "Are you selling your goat at all today? I need a good goat for breeding purposes."

Johnnyboy smiled from ear to ear. "I sure am selling my goat." He continued to tell his inebriated potential buyer what a wonderful goat Jacinta was. "She is a young goat, and she has had many kids in the past few years, and she is in fine health."

After haggling about a final price for Jacinta, they agreed on a particular sum of money. Having put the money in the safety of his back pocket, Johnnyboy handed over Jacinta to her new owner. He wished the buyer well and ran off in the opposite direction, rubbing his hands together, delighted that his plan to sell Jacinta was realised and he had money in his pocket to prove it.

Mum often wondered about Paudeen's original family, but he never spoke about them. Maybe he'd had a falling out with them or they had all passed away. She knew his father's name or his grandfather's name was Patrick. In Ireland, there is a custom whereby your eldest son was ever and always named after either one. Hence his name, Paudeen – little Patrick.

As night fell fast, he got up and rushed out the back door.

Concerned for his welfare, I turned to Mum. "Where is he going?"

"He will sleep on a bed of straw in the old calf shed across the road."

"In a bed of straw, like Baby Jesus?" I exclaimed.

"Well, yes, similar to where Baby Jesus slept." She gave my shoulder a reassuring rub. "As soon as the light of day breaks, Paudeen will continue his travels, but he is sure to return again in the next five to six months, as he always does."

Before Mum went to bed that night, she wrapped some buttered soda bread in brown paper, then filled a lemonade bottle with milk. With the aid of a flashlamp, she went across the road and left them, including a pair of clean socks, inside the shed door for Paudeen.

Perplexed by his plight, and because it was a freezing winter's evening, Ted and I found it hard to sleep in our warm beds. But, again, Mum assured us that he was a freeborn man, who liked to travel.

"He is happy with his lifestyle, and he would not change it for the world."

My brother and I met many interesting people during our life on the farm, but few were as memorable as Paudeen.

The Christmas Season

On 21 December, the shortest day of the year, our preparations for Christmas began in earnest. Nano always said it got brighter by a 'cock step' each evening from this day onwards. My brother and I were excited about Christmas and the onset of brighter evenings, but we didn't care for the chores that had to be done before the big day arrived.

Before the clean-up began, Mum and Nano had already posted their colourful Christmas greeting cards, to friends, neighbours, and to relatives living in the United Kingdom, America, and Australia. But, more importantly, our letters to Santy, as we called him, had already been posted.

The cleaning and tidying of our kitchen began with the concrete floor being scrubbed from one side to the other. We didn't have much furniture, only our big wooden table, *súgán* chairs and a wooden fireside bench, which were all scrubbed spotless.

With that done, the walls were painted dark green and the doors and ceiling were painted cream. All of the outside walls were whitewashed – even the animal sheds got a lick of whitewash. And, of course, the chimney was swept in preparation for the arrival of the man himself. Grandpa began this procedure by pushing a holly bush up and down the inside of the chimney to loosen the soot before he and Pop swept it.

The wooden box radio, placed on a little table in one corner of the room, got a quick dusting before the crib was placed upon it. Our kitchen was decorated with an abundance of red-berry holly, which was also placed into any crevice or on any picture that could support a twig. The Sacred Heart picture got special attention, with small candles placed under it on a shelf to add to the glowing red light already illuminating it. Multicoloured honeycomb paper decorations were strung criss-crossed on the kitchen ceiling, held in place with thumbtacks. A green, red, and gold decoration that fanned out into a bell shape, fixed with metal tags and hung in the middle of the ceiling, was my favourite one of all. When someone opened the back door, I watched it swirl around and around with gusto from the incoming draft.

Mum filled an old paint tin with sand. To disguise it, she decorated it with red and green Christmas-themed paper and tied twine around the wrapping to keep it in place. Afterwards, she pressed a large red candle into the sand and duly placed it on the front windowsill.

Every evening, she lit that thick red candle, and I feared it would set fire to the white net curtains on the window. Mum went to great lengths to explain to me that the candle was necessary, as it lit the way for the holy family, but this did nothing to allay my fears.

Other times, Mum would fetch an old dark-green wine bottle from the cupboard. She pared the end of a red candle and stuck it in the neck of the bottle. It wasn't quite as glamorous as the decorated paint tin, but it was fun to see the excess lumpy and bumpy wax gathering on the sides of the bottle. Mum's last job before going to bed each night was to make sure all the candles were well and truly blown out.

My brother got the task of tidying the pathway leading from the roadside to our front door and of course as always I helped him. Not that it needed it, as anyone who ever visited our house entered by the back door, with the exception of the postman, and the odd government official.

Along each side of this pathway grew a fuchsia hedge, which we took immense pleasure in trimming to a height well lower than was necessary. We took turns using a rather large steel scissors-like gadget with wooden handles – a handheld hedge trimmer. There was method in our madness, as the lower we cut the hedge, the less often we had to trim it.

As was usual at Christmas time, Mum and Pop went to our nearest big town to "bring home the Christmas". This was a phrase we heard often in the weeks leading up to Christmas Day. Back then, it meant to buy whatever groceries and toys were needed for the festivities.

Mum always got excited about this trip to town, as she'd saved as many pennies as possible during the year. She wanted to make the Christmas season special for us children, and she wrote a long list the night before the big excursion, with the likes of raisins, currants, sultanas, and cinnamon to make the Christmas cake and other groceries, as well as porter and a bottle of Irish whiskey for the men to drink, Sandeman port for the women, and lemonade aplenty for us children. Our toys, of course, were purchased that day, too, but were hidden out of sight, until Santy arrived with them on Christmas morning.

Pop was excited for the trip, too, and he set off with Mum on the journey just before midday in the car. While Mum did the Christmas shopping, he had a legitimate excuse to spend this time drinking pints of porter and chatting with other like-minded men in an establishment known well to them.

Mum's shopping trip took about three hours, and when she was ready to go home, she went to the public house and found Pop somewhat inebriated. He asked her to sit down and have a *tosheen* – a little drop of alcohol. Needless to say, Mum refused. She then took a deep breath and didn't say another word, as this was not the usual carry on for her husband. I overheard her tell Nano all about it and that Pop was driving erratically on the way home from town, sometimes even on the wrong side of the road. She also told Nano that she blessed herself a few times and asked the good man above to bring them safely home. Once indoors, she drank a big mug of tea to settle her nerves.

Ted, our sisters and I loved it when Mum made the Christmas cake. But arguments ensued as to who would get to lick the big cream bowl when she'd finished her work of art. Once made, the cake was stored in a round tin until Christmas day. A delightful aroma of cinnamon wafted from the tin when Mum opened it every now and then to check if the cake was okay. To this day, I love the aromatic smell of this spice in the kitchen at Christmas time.

Some people made Christmas cakes well in advance of the big day. But not our mum. No, she made ours two weeks beforehand, and from her own special recipe, and it was delicious.

Bob, our local shopkeeper, presented us and each family in Gorse Valley and surroundings areas with a Christmas box, as a reward for loyalty during the year. A lovely gesture, which epitomised the spirit of Christmas back then. It consisted of a huge bag of tea and sugar and an enormous tin of scrumptious biscuits.

One of my favourite memories from Christmas Eve is Josh arriving on his big black bike with a bundle of Christmas cards. After leaving mail in several households on his five-mile postal run, he was always a tad merry, having had a drop of alcohol here and there. Mum invited him in for tea and Christmas cake. As our house was his last stop and he was in no rush, several hours later and with a little more of the hard stuff consumed, Pop had to give him a lift home in the car, with his bike squeezed in the boot.

Mum arranged our latest bundle of Christmas cards with those we had already received. It was amazing to see them strung up with twine in three long rows over the mantlepiece. They arrived from relatives and friends living locally, and from the United Kingdom, America, and Australia, and were all shapes and sizes, bearing greetings such as 'Merry Christmas', 'Season's Greetings', 'Let it Snow', and were adorned with Santy Hats, Reindeers, and much more.

Our next important task for Christmas Eve was to attend Mass at midnight. Dressed in our best clothes, we went to church in Pop's car. In the church, the highlight for us children was the crib, built of wood by local men and set up near the altar. It was covered in straw and holly, and a glowing light illuminated the inside of it. Mesmerised, I gazed in to see where Baby Jesus, wrapped in swaddling clothes, was laid in a manger of straw, with Mary and Joseph at his side. They were surrounded by the three wise men, bearing gifts of gold, frankincense, and myrrh. Behind him, a donkey, oxen, and sheep gathered, appearing to breathe warmth on Baby Jesus's tiny body. We all knelt in front of it, prayed a little and lit some candles.

Afterwards, the litany of Christmas Eve Mass, prayers went on for what seemed like an eternity to us children. But we did enjoy the carol singing, and Mum went into soprano mode once again.

When at last we arrived back home, Ted and I legged it up the stairs to our beds. After tucking us in, Mum assured us that Santy would arrive during the night with our Christmas gifts.

Christmas morning arrived and we skipped down the stairs, excited to see what gifts Santy had left for us. A wooden train set and a book for Ted stood by the fireside in a neat cardboard box, covered in Christmas wrapping paper. Our sisters got board games – Ludo, and Snakes and Ladders – and books. Nano left a big juicy orange for each of us children, hung in stockings on the mantelpiece. Oranges were a luxury back then, and the Christmas stockings were not those we see today, being quality, handknitted knee-high socks, which she crafted for us. She also left us a two-penny bag of sweets each. We never had a Christmas tree, nor did we miss it.

But the biggest surprise of all was that Santy left a walkie-talkie doll for me. She, too, was nicely wrapped with Christmas paper and red bows.

It was several years later that I discovered who left this beautiful Christmas gift. Our Aunt Peig in the UK, Uncle Peter's wife, organised it for me, as I was her godchild, but Mum and Pop pretended my gift came from Santy. How lucky was I to receive a much-treasured doll, one that could walk and talk, and the likes of which was unheard of in Gorse Valley. Her hair was blonde, tied back in pigtails, and she had icy-blue eyes and was outfitted in a red dress and black shoes.

With the morning farm chores done, Mum spent the best part of two hours cooking up a mouth-watering Christmas dinner. She had prepared the goose the evening before and this task was done with the utmost attention to detail.

Firstly, it was Pop's job to remove the entrails of the goose, which he did in double-quick time. Mum singed any remaining small feathers and cleaned her all over. She made the most amazing potato and onion stuffing and stuffed the body of the goose, through her rear end. She then sewed this part of the bird's anatomy with a darning needle and strong thread, to make sure none of the stuffing escaped during the cooking process. I remember the mouth-watering smell of the goose cooking, with the stuffing, which created a ravishing hunger for all eight of us.

Christmas dinner was served in our parlour, which was also decorated from top to bottom with all sorts of Christmas decorations. The shining, floral, gilt-edged china Delftware, including large serving platters, were placed on the grand parlour table. We sat at this and feasted like kings on stuffed goose, potatoes, carrots, delicious gravy, and finished off our meal with custard and jelly, a real delight for us children.

Afterwards, it was time for our visitors to arrive – some neighbours, including Mrs O'Brien. We told stories and danced around the kitchen floor to the sound of traditional Irish music booming from our wooden box radio. Pints of porter, whiskey, Sandeman port, and copious amounts of tea were drunk by the adults, with lemonade for the children. A large plate of homemade Christmas cake was always at the ready on the kitchen table.

Once our neighbours and Mrs O'Brien returned to their respective homes, our farm chores would beckon in the evening. When finished and back indoors, we chatted by the cosy fireside, reminisced about our Christmas Day and about Santy's kindness for the wonderful gifts he brought to the younger members of our family.

Every year on Saint Stephen's Day, a Wren Boy event took place in rural Ireland.

Crowds of boys and men began their shenanigans by capturing an innocent bird on Christmas evening. A poor little wren, the king of all birds, was chased down from hedgerows or the eaves of old houses or sheds, then captured and killed by the Wren Boys.

The next day, the 26th of December, the feast day of Saint Stephen, they dressed in scary or straw costumes and wore masks on their faces as a disguise. Having placed the dead wren on top of a stick, they went around knocking on each door in the neighbourhood, playing blaring traditional music and chanting, while asking for money to bury the wren.

This dreaded event was one that scared the heart and soul out of Ted and me, and we hid upstairs in our bedroom until we knew that the Wren Boys had left our home and gone on to a neighbouring house. Our family, and I am sure there were many others who had a love of little birds, avoided taking part in such gatherings like the plague back then.

While there were many twisted tales and traditions of the Wren Boys, it was generally believed, through folklore handed down from one generation to the next, that the wren was responsible for the death of Saint Stephen. It was thought the saint was hiding in bushes from his enemies and the chattering of the wren alerted them to his whereabouts. Saint Stephen, the first Christian martyr, was accused of blasphemy and stoned to death by his captors. The Wren Boys believed that the little bird should receive the same fate as Saint Stephen.

Once they'd finished going from house to house and collecting money, they did indeed bury the wren. Then they began celebrating with dancing and singing, at a given location, with drink aplenty for the adults.

Thankfully, now, a much milder version of the Wren Boys takes place, where an effigy of the wren is used and the little bird is no longer captured and stoned to death. Mostly, the proceeds of the event go to some deserving charity.

The Christmas season didn't end there, as *Nollag na mBan* – Women's Christmas – was next on the calendar. It was an important occasion when I was growing up, and a lovely Irish tradition, a day when hardworking mothers and grandmothers got a well-deserved rest after all their preparations for the festivities. It occurs each year on the 6th of January, the feast of the Epiphany, and is celebrated in some Irish homes to this day. It also marks the end of the Christmas season.

I remember well that on this day Pop was supposed to take over the chores of our home, cleaning, cooking meals, and giving Mum and Nano an opportunity to visit relatives or friends, to have long chats and copious amounts of tea and cake, without having to worry about any domestic responsibilities. To say the least, Pop was not accustomed to any of these indoor duties, and I often heard Nano say, "He couldn't even boil an egg to save himself from starvation."

Cait glared at him when she saw his paltry efforts at sweeping the kitchen floor. Kind-hearted Elizabeth helped him as much as she could, peeling the potatoes and carrots for our dinner. Ted and I remained quiet, sitting by the blazing fire, while Grandpa told us stories of his boyhood Christmas days.

Pop cooked our meal, and though it was not deliciously tasty like Mum's dinners, we ate it all, then rowed in washing the dishes and tidying up. Next, we helped Pop take down the Christmas decorations, and when we had finished packing them away for the next year, our kitchen felt bare. We were all a little sad that the Christmas season had come to an end.

But I was glad, and I am sure Ted was, too, that the goose Mum bought from Ada no longer hung on the back door. I am also happy to report that many of these Christmas traditions have survived in my family to this day.

The Stations

The only other time I remember our home being cleaned like it was for Christmas, was for the Stations. Indeed, that was also the only other time our more-or-less defunct but grand parlour room was used, as it was the fancy room – the good room of our home.

This event dates back to when the Penal Laws forbade Catholic priests from saying Mass in public. To get around this law, Mass was secretly celebrated in people's homes, and a breakfast was served to all attendees.

After many years went by and the Penal Laws were repealed, the custom continued, especially in rural areas, including County Kerry. This event was better known to all in Gorse Valley and most rural areas as the Stations, which differs from the Stations of the Cross, a prayer ritual that takes place in Catholic churches on Fridays during Lent.

It was a time when people were obliged by their parish priest to take turns at holding a Mass service in their home. Our house was the fifth in the townland; therefore, it was our turn every fifth year to host the event, and it could take place in spring or autumn, depending on the priest's schedule.

The Stations was not met with great enthusiasm by the hosts of the Mass, as it tended to be a stressful time. Normal family and farming life stood still for the few days leading up to it, with lots of cleaning, preparing, and making sure everything indoors and outdoors was exactly right. I remember Mum and Nano being stressed when it was our family's turn to host the event.

On the appointed day, and before the priest arrived at our house for the ceremony, we children were immaculately dressed in our Sunday-best clothing. Mum gave a strict warning to Ted, our sisters and me to be on our best behaviour – with no jig acting, no laughing or giggling, and to pay attention to the priest and say our prayers. Sally had no idea what was going on, either, as she was banished to the cowshed lest she bark during the ceremony. Betty the cat was once again chased to the other end of the haggard, as she had a habit of being a nuisance around the kitchen.

Our neighbours from the other four households, including their children, arrived first, followed a brief time later by the priest. When he arrived, Pop took his suitcase to the parlour room, where he vested before hearing confessions from anyone brave enough to avail themselves of his absolution and penance, after which he said Mass from a makeshift altar placed at the top end of our kitchen table. The altar was covered in snowy-white bedsheets, with the finest of linen draped over them. It was then adorned with a crucifix, glowing candles, and a vase of flowers.

The priest said the Mass in the ancient Latin language, and the congregation mostly said their own prayers, fingering their rosary beads. Holy Communion was offered to those who wished to receive it.

There wasn't enough seating for everyone, and most children stood throughout the ceremony, with some devout men down on one knee, using their folded caps as a cushion.

Then it was time for the priest to attend to financial matters. A collection box was handed around the gathering for his upkeep and to help the host of the following year's Station Mass financially. Everyone gave whatever they could afford. One person gave a heap of change, which evoked mutterings and slagging within the congregation that he must have been out singing in some town, with his hand held out for alms.

Afterwards, the priest, being revered, got the finest feast at the head of the parlour table, prepared meticulously by Mum and Nano. They had already set the dining room table with white linen cloth and napkins and, similar to our Christmas Day dinner, the food was served to him in shining, floral, gilt-edged china Delftware, including large serving platters and silver cutlery. The priest's food consisted of two fried eggs, rashers, sausages, and black and white pudding, served with freshly made soda bread. Red and white wine was available if he wished to indulge. Pop and Danjoe were also treated to the same breakfast, as they accompanied the priest during the meal.

One particular item on the parlour table interested me the most – a bowl of cubed sugar, purchased by Mum to adorn the table and enhance the taste of the priest's breakfast tea. Nano was much in agreement with the cubed sugar being served for the officiant's tea, as, of course, she had worked in the big houses and was well versed in matters of grandeur.

Everyone else awaited their turn to be served, and ate a more modest breakfast of boiled eggs, with buttered soda bread and jam. Nano had baked three amazing loaves of currant bread, which were buttered and scoffed in no time by all and sundry. Best of all, though, was that jelly and custard was given to all children present, which I thoroughly enjoyed.

The priest left after an hour or more when he'd finished his fine feast. Once he'd gone, Ted, Cait, Elizabeth and I didn't have to stand as stiff as pokers in reverence anymore. We could talk and giggle to our heart's content, with no restrictions. The merriment began for all present with music, dancing, and storytelling. Lemonade was plentiful for us children, with an abundance of sherry, tea, and porter available for the adults.

Apart from having fun with Ted and the neighbouring children, the best part of the gathering for me was when I grabbed a handful of cubed sugar from the parlour room table and munched away on them when the adults were distracted.

The merriment continued well into the small hours of the morning. When all neighbours had left and gone home, Mum and Nano, though exhausted, could breathe a sigh of relief. Their Station plans had gone well, and they didn't have to go through the stress of hosting such an event for another five years.

Aunt Maureen Comes Home

Mum could not contain her excitement when Josh arrived one fine April morning with a letter from her sister Maureen in America.

Dear Kate,

I have enormous pleasure in letting you know that I will finally be arriving in Gorse Valley on Wednesday the 1st day of June. It has been way too long since I visited my homeland and I very much look forward to seeing you all. Unfortunately, my time in Ireland will be short, as my nursing schedule is very tight for several months, and I can only stay for a five-day vacation.

My good friend Judith is accompanying me, and I hope this is okay with you and Jimmy. She has heard so much about Ireland from me through the years and cannot wait to see it for herself.

Take care, love and best wishes, Maureen x

Well, the preparations for Aunt Maureen and Judith's visit began almost there and then. It was a relief that the painting of the walls didn't have to be done, as that chore had already been completed for the Christmas season. Everything in the kitchen was cleaned. Cobwebs, dust, and soot from the open fire were swiped clean with a goose-feather duster.

I heard Pop say, "If anyone stood still for a second in the kitchen, they're likely to get a swipe of the feather duster from either Mum or Nano."

As well as getting a general tidy up, everything in our parlour room was also dusted and cleaned, as that was where Aunt Maureen and Judith were going to sleep. Mum borrowed a double bed from a kind neighbour and took great delight in dressing it with gleaming white sheets, pillows, and a floral bedspread. Within a few weeks, all preparations were complete and ready for the arrival of our two visitors. We were all excited beyond belief, Mum in particular.

The evening before their arrival, the four of us children got haircuts, carried out with army-like precision by Pop with his shiny silver scissors. Our galvanised bath was put into action, and the same bathing ritual occurred in front of the fire as it did on Saturday nights in preparation for Sunday Mass. Mum laid out our best clothes – our Sunday clothes – ready for the next morning, when we had finished our farm chores.

All arose early Wednesday morning in anticipation of our guests' arrival. Pop drove to Shannon Airport to meet them, and while he was away, the rest of us got all the outdoor work done. For the umpteenth time, Mum told the four of us children to be on our best behaviour, not to speak until spoken to, and to have manners in our guests' presence. She rarely had to raise her voice to any one of us, her stern sideways glance being enough to convey her disapproval if we misbehaved.

With no sign of anyone for ages, our eagerness waned a little, and it wasn't until they arrived that we discovered the flight they were on from San Francisco to Shannon had been delayed by two hours. But when they did arrive, much to the relief of Mum, Nano, and Grandpa, there were greetings, hugs, and kisses exchanged by all and sundry. Mum and Aunt Maureen shed tears of joy at seeing each other for the first time in sixteen years.

"Once I stepped on Irish soil, I felt at home," Aunt Maureen said.

Mum assured her and Judith that they were welcome to Ireland, and particularly so to Gorse Valley.

Aunt Maureen was tall and slim, with permed blonde hair, and she wore a bright-pink flowery dress. Judith was low-sized, with auburn hair, and wore a tan-colour jacket and matching skirt.

Everyone sat around the table and had dinner together, which Mum and Nano had prepared earlier. We chatted nonstop for an hour or more, updating Aunt Maureen about everything that was happening in Gorse Valley. I found it difficult to understand her American accent to begin with, but I got used to it after a while. Judith didn't say much during this time but listened with interest to what we were talking about.

Though this was a very joyous time for Mum and Aunt Maureen, it was very much tinged with sadness too, as Nanny Margaret had passed on five months earlier in January. I have no recollection of her passing, as I had whooping cough and was cared for at home by Nano during her funeral.

Mum showed our guests to their room and helped them with their suitcases. They seemed a tad surprised by the fact that they had to share a double bed, but that was the best arrangement Mum was able to make. They emerged from the parlour a brief time later with gifts for each one of us, as well as sumptuous USA-brand sweets for us children.

"May I use the bathroom?" Judith asked Mum.

"Oh yes, of course you may. Just go out the back door, turn left, and it is in the old shed with the green door."

"Oh, golly gosh, it's okay," Judith said, "I will use the bathroom upstairs."

"No, no, you don't understand, we don't have an upstairs bathroom."

Aunt Maureen intervened, "The only bathroom available, Judith, is the one Kate just mentioned."

Judith proceeded out the back, to the green-door bathroom. When she returned indoors, she looked somewhat bemused.

"There is only a bucket and newspaper in that shed," she exclaimed, with furrowed brow.

"Oh yes, yes, that is our new bathroom," Mum replied, standing with one hand on her hip and her chin held high. "We upgraded it recently."

Aunt Maureen politely explained to her that this was rural Ireland, and there were no indoor flushing toilets. Bathroom and wash facilities were quite different here than in urban and city areas or in the USA.

Judith was blissfully unaware that, up to a short while ago, our toilet facilities were of a lesser standard and convenience. When the need for a bathroom visit arose, the haggard was the place to go, and everyone in our family had their own private nook there. If someone had an urgent need to use such facilities during the darkness of night, elegant and portable chamber pots were at the ready underneath all beds.

While we did our evening farm chores, Aunt Maureen, Judith and Nano sat by the open fire chatting to beat the band. Afterwards, we all had currant bread and tea and chatted more until it was bedtime.

The next morning, after having their breakfast, our two guests decided they would go for a swim in the sea. The long and wide expanse of deep-blue sea was easy to see from the front window of our parlour, and it must have seemed enticing to them.

Accompanied by Cait, Elizabeth, Ted and me, they headed across the road and down the boreen. We hadn't gone too far when Judith yelled. She had twisted her ankle on the rough stones of the boreen. She wasn't used to such terrain, and I remember thinking if she wasn't wearing those red high-heeled shoes, she wouldn't have injured herself in the first place.

We all returned to our house, with Judith hobbling and in pain. But Aunt Maureen knew how to care for her foot, as she had extensive nursing experience. Judith sat for the remainder of the day beside the fire, with her injured leg on a low stool.

Aunt Maureen was determined to have a swim in the briny waters of the Irish sea, as she had been looking forward to doing so for a long time. Off we went again down to the strand, but this time minus Judith. Once we arrived, our aunt took a running jump across the sand and landed in the water.

"Ooh, my goodness gracious me," she screamed, "this water is petrifyingly cold."

In all the years she spent living in America, it seemed she'd forgotten how cold the waters of the Atlantic Ocean could be. Nevertheless, she persevered and swam a little, watched by the four of us children.

Later that evening, our entire family and our guests relaxed in the kitchen, playing cards and chatting. Uncle Bill joined us, as he was anxious to see his eldest sister. Grandpa kept quiet, as he couldn't understand Aunt Maureen and Judith's American accents, and, likewise, they couldn't understand his thick Kerry brogue. Pop stayed a bit quiet, too, as it appeared he disliked Judith. But he dared not utter a word, or he would get the brunt of Mum's sharp tongue.

The next afternoon our visitors, accompanied by Mum, went to see Mrs O'Brien, with Judith still hobbling a bit.

"They were amazed at the beauty of her thatched cottage," Mum said after as she related how the visit went, "and they found it hard to comprehend that she left the USA in her eightieth year. Aunt Maureen was disturbed by the fact that she was left with no option but to leave for Ireland after that horrible break in."

They chatted about matters in the USA, and Mum served them up tea and homemade cake. But their visit to Mrs

O'Brien was short lived, as she whispered to Mum that she was tired and not feeling too well.

The following morning, Aunt Maureen and Judith left to spend the day in our nearest big town, as they needed to buy gifts to take back to the USA. Pop needed to buy some animal feed and had some other matters to attend to in town, so they all went together in his Ford Prefect.

Mum was concerned about Mrs O'Brien. She spent the day toing and froing to her house, making hot drinks and attending to her every need. To her delight, by evening time, she appeared to be improving.

Maureen, Judith, and Pop arrived back after their daytrip to town, and they, too, were concerned about Mrs O'Brien, wondering if she had improved. Mum wasted no time updating them.

Once they had their evening meal finished – cooked by Nano – they got busy packing their suitcases. Their flight back to the USA was leaving quite early the next morning. Having bought many gifts during their trip to town, their suitcases were bulging almost beyond capacity. Cait and Elizabeth helped Aunt Maureen and Judith to close each case by standing on them, and they succeeded in closing and locking each one after much effort.

Before Ted, our sisters and I went to bed, we bade Aunt Maureen and Judith a sad goodbye. Our aunt assured us that she would return from the USA again soon, and not to feel sad. Nano and Grandpa also said farewell to them and wished them a safe flight home. Mum and her sister hugged each other tight, heartbroken to be parting once again, with tears streaming down their cheeks.

The next morning at dawn, Pop drove the ladies back to Shannon Airport, and it wasn't long before they were winging their way back to the USA. When he arrived home, he assured Mum that all had gone according to plan, and that all good things must come to an end.

It took another decade before Aunt Maureen made it back to Ireland, and by then so much had changed in all our lives. We no longer lived in Gorse Valley, Nano and Grandpa had become old and infirm, and Mum and Pop's hair had gained silver hues as they struggled with the challenges of farming life as well as rearing and educating four children.

Our aunt had suffered some serious health issues in the meantime, which necessitated her taking ongoing medication.

By this time Cait, Elizabeth, Ted and I had finished our education and were busy with work and social activities. But, however occupied we were, we always had a warm welcome for our Aunt Maureen and loved to spend quality time with her reminiscing about times past.

Wake and Funeral

Danjoe arrived at our house really early one summer morning all perturbed. Though he thought he was out of earshot of us children, I heard him whispering to Mum.

"Kate, I tried to check up on Mrs O'Brien, but the door is locked. I knocked several times and there was no answer."

Mum, Pop, and Danjoe hurried across the road to Mrs O'Brien's cottage, and she later told Nano that there wasn't a sound to be heard, except for the barking of her little dog Toby. And on inspection of the back of her cottage, they could see through a gap in the curtains of her bedroom that she was in her bed.

Mum ran back to our house and grabbed a spare key to Mrs O'Brien's cottage from our kitchen windowsill. I noticed that Mum's face was flushed and her hands were trembling. The three of them entered her cottage and couldn't believe their eyes on finding their lovely elderly neighbour lifeless in her bed.

Mum contacted the local Garda, who arrived sometime later on his bicycle. She also contacted Doctor Moore, who turned up in a grand swanky car. On examination, he confirmed Mrs O'Brien's death and that she had died approximately six hours previously. Mum and Danjoe were upset that she'd died alone, without anyone to hold her hand while she took her last breaths in this world.

Mrs O'Brien had no living relatives – not even in the USA. With the priest's help, Mum began planning for her wake and funeral, and the wake took place that evening at five o'clock.

Nano told Ted and me that, with the help of two or three local women, Mum laid out Mrs O'Brien in her bed, in a flowery nightgown, and placed her rosary beads between her joined hands. They dressed her bed in brilliant-white cotton sheets and a snowy white bedspread. A crucifix and some small candles were placed on a tall narrow table beside her bed. Mum stopped the clock on the hour the doctor said she died and drew the heavy curtains on her window. Within a short time, everything was ready, with Mrs O'Brien's room and kitchen cleaned from top to bottom.

Mum asked Ted and me if we would like to see Mrs O'Brien laid out and say a prayer beside her bed?

"Oh, no, no, Mum," I said, "we would prefer to remember her as she always was, with her black clothing, and her bright flowery-pink scarf on her head. We will stay in her kitchen."

Meanwhile, Pop and Danjoe had bought drink and groceries in our local shop for those who came to pay their respects to Mrs O'Brien. Mum and the local women prepared a mammoth amount of food and set it out on the kitchen table, and all was ready for the wake later that evening.

I recall it well as, at that point in the proceedings, Pop nearly had a hissy fit on remembering that his shoes were in the cobbler's being mended. Holes had worn on the soles of his shiny black leather shoes, the only footwear he had to wear to Mrs O'Brien's funeral the next day. Without another word, he jumped in his car and collected them from the shoemaker three townlands away.

The priest arrived and I heard him whispering prayers in Mrs O'Brien's bedroom. Those who came to pay their respects to her, and they came in droves, also prayed for her. Afterwards, they exchanged story snippets about what she meant to them, and they conveyed their love for her, while partaking in the food set out for them on the kitchen table.

As it was getting late, the mourners and everyone else went home, except for Pop and Danjoe. They kept vigil over Mrs O'Brien's body throughout the night, as was the custom, lest it fall prey to evil spirits.

The funeral carriage arrived at the cottage at nine o'clock sharp the next morning, a stately, elegant hearse, drawn by two shiny black draught horses with bobbing plumes on their heads. Two black-clad undertakers guided them, each with a bowler hat on his head. After a while, they emerged from the cottage with Mrs O'Brien's body in a teak casket, with the lid closed. When the coffin was loaded onto the carriage, they were ready for the journey to the church.

Both undertakers sat up front on the funeral carriage, and one drove the horses with leather reins. It moved at a slow, steady pace, then picked up a little speed as the horses began an even trot.

It was one of the saddest sights that my big brother and I had ever witnessed. Our hearts sank as we watched our lovely neighbour Mrs O'Brien leaving in the funeral carriage, for the last ever time. Ted put his arms around me, and tears streamed down both of our faces while we watched the cortege until it disappeared out of sight along the narrow winding road.

We would never see Mrs O'Brien again or do daily chores for her. There was only one consolation: we inherited her little dog Toby, who we took great care of from that day onwards.

Ted and I heard Mum tell Nano that, as the cortege approached the church, the funeral bell began to toll a slow peal. She also said that, at this time, she got extremely emotional at the loss of their lovely neighbour, and her handkerchief was soaked from her tears."

Mrs O'Brien's funeral Mass and burial went well, according to Mum. The priest said some kind words about the deceased, and mentioned the circumstances in which she had left the USA and how locals welcomed her when she arrived in Gorse Valley. Danjoe was given the great honour of delivering Mrs O'Brien's eulogy, which he found hard to finish without becoming emotional a few times. At the end, some hymns were sung.

The mourners formed a procession behind the horse-drawn carriage as it took Mrs O'Brien to her final resting place. Mum mentioned that more prayers were said over her casket at the cemetery, and it got a final blessing from the priest before being lowered into her grave.

And after leaving the cemetery, the mourners headed for the local public house to celebrate the life of the dearly departed Mrs O'Brien. Some continued the celebration well into the wee hours of the morning.

I remember Mrs O'Brien with fondness – a lovely lady, always thankful for any act of kindness that was bestowed upon her.

"BE THE THINGS YOU LOVED MOST
ABOUT THE PEOPLE WHO ARE GONE"

– Unknown

Government Resettlement Scheme

When the new Irish Free State Government was established in December 1922, they knew that if it was to maintain social stability, they had to tackle the enormous issue of land. As a result, it passed the 1923 Land Act, which gave huge powers to the Irish Land Commission. They purchased the estates of the gentry and grazier families in Dublin, Kildare, along with other counties in the east of the country and divided them into smaller holding.

The aim of the scheme was to resettle farmers and their families from the west and southwest of Ireland to larger holdings and better-quality land in the eastern counties. At that time, the demand for whole milk and the price paid to farmers for it was far greater in the east than it was along the western seaboard of Ireland.

Much of Pop's twenty acres in Kerry was of inferior quality – stony, boggy, and rush-filled. After deep and thorough discussions with Mum, Nano, and Grandpa, and taking into consideration the fact that it was hard to make a living in Gorse Valley, he applied to the Irish Land Commission for the resettlement scheme. There was a rigorous selection process to go through and not everyone who applied was successful, and the paperwork for the scheme took well over twelve months to complete from the date of application.

After an agonising wait and much stress and anxiety for my parents and grandparents, the deal was finalised. Pop surrendered our small farm holding to the Irish Land Commission, and they in turn resettled us to a bigger and more productive farm holding in County Dublin. It was agreed that Pop would pay them rent for many years to cover the price difference between the smaller and larger holdings.

I have vivid memories of Mum packing food for Pop on a bright sunny June morning. She explained to me that he was going on a long journey in his car to Dublin.

"But why is Pop going to Dublin?" I asked.

"He is going to see our new home and farm."

"I want to see it too."

"You will, Maggie, you will see it very soon."

The date for our move from Gorse Valley to County Dublin was set in stone: 21 June 1959, the longest day of the year. And almost overnight – or so it seemed to us children – our migration became a reality. Cait and Elizabeth didn't want to leave the friends they had spent many years with, and I didn't want to move and leave Neddy or any of our animals in Gorse Valley. Ted was adamant that he was not moving and leaving all of our animals behind.

"Maggie, this is all Pop's fault," he said, his face red with temper. "He is mean, and we have to move because it suits him."

"No, no, Ted, don't let Pop hear you say that. He'll be angry with you."

"Oh ... okay, but it's still unfair."

Just then, Mum came into our bedroom to say our night prayers with us. Ted tried to speak but was choked with tears. I told Mum what was upsetting him and she explained that we would all like our new home in County Dublin, and that we would have a better quality of life.

"Cheer up now, Ted, all will be fine, and we most definitely will not be leaving any of our animals behind."

His face brightened at that news. "Okay, Mum, okay."

Contented, we both fell fast asleep before Mum had a chance to say our prayers with us.

While Grandpa had resigned himself to moving, Nano changed her mind at one stage and told us all that she was staying. For days before we moved, her eyes were bloodshot red, and the white cotton handkerchief she held in her hand was soaked with tears, but there was no option available to her – she had to move with us.

The evening before we moved, Ted and I, accompanied by Sally, herded our cows from one of our fields – our furze field – and along the road to our farmyard, as we often did.

This particular part of our holding was nestled at the foot of the mountain, taking up about five acres. Picture a field of furze bushes, in spring and early summertime, displaying a beautiful array of yellow flowers. Their natural aroma was breathtaking, and we spent many hours playing hide and seek around them.

A stream wound its way from the top of the mountain and widened out into a slow-moving stony river, which ran along one side of the field. Most times, Sally watched from the riverbank, always anxious, appearing to know that what we were doing was a little risky as we dared each other to cross the river from one side to the other. Good balance was necessary to step from one slimy green stone to the next in our wellington boots, and an unplanned dunk in the river was often the result of a moment's distraction.

"You cross first, Maggie," Ted would say.

"No, no, Ted, I went first the last day, now it's your turn to go first."

"Hmm, okay," he said, not too happy at the prospect of ending up in the water.

Even though we were young and innocent, tears streamed down our faces when it dawned on us that we would never do this chore again. We patted Sally on the head and hugged her, as it appeared she was also aware of the impending life-changing event.

Moving to County Dublin

Moving home at any time is one of the most arduous and stressful tasks. But when this included many farm animals and a huge amount of farming equipment, it brought the experience to another level of stress altogether. A life-changing chapter – a fresh beginning.

To say Mum and our grandparents were looking forward to this day with apprehension was a total understatement. But with Pop having already viewed our new farm holding in County Dublin, he assured them that everything would be fine.

Packing of our belongings began a week before our move, when eager relatives and neighbours arrived, willing to help and make our move as easy as possible.

Our kitchen became a scene like that of a packaging factory. Each box had to be packed with care, all its contents being labelled so we knew where to find everything when we arrived at our new home. The ladies packed all of our clothes, shoes, Delftware, furniture, and everything else in our home, as we left nothing behind. Even our beds had to be packed last minute before we left. Ted was ten years old at this time, I was nine, and our sisters Cait and Elizabeth were a little older still. We were mesmerised at it all but, as children, did not comprehend the impact it would have on the rest of our lives.

One solitary item that needed packing – our tall china cabinet – stood empty in the parlour, waiting for Mum's inspiration on how it would fit with everything. When everyone was outside, I climbed up with the aid of a chair to make sure there was nothing left in the cabinet, especially a little doll that I loved, given to me by Mrs O'Brien. Next thing, and because it was empty, it toppled forward and hit the wooden floor with an almighty bang, with me pinned beneath it. Mum and Ted heard my screams and ran to the parlour to see what happened. They lifted the cabinet off me and were relieved to see that I was unhurt, apart from my childish ego, which took a battering that day.

Outdoors, the men packed all the farm equipment into big wooden crates. Our donkey and pony carts had to be packed too. As all equipment had to be disassembled, it was difficult and time-consuming work. It didn't help much when, on three of these supposed to be summer days, rain poured from the heavens and the farmyard became a sodden mess, with the haggard turned into a mass of boot-sucking mud. At least Nano's tea and buttery scones softened the impact of their work.

That evening, there was no time for a neighbourly get-together, as Pop, Mum, and our grandparents still had a lot of farm chores and other work to do. Indeed, no sleep was had by them that particular night.

Next morning – the dreaded morning for our family – our cows were milked at the much earlier time of 5am. Afterwards, pandemonium ensued when two monstrous lorries arrived. All livestock on our farm, mooing, neighing, and braying, were loaded onto them, including Neddy. Pop had previously sold our sheep and pigs to make the move simpler.

Our farm equipment, including our tractor, were loaded onto a third lorry, and all furniture pieces were loaded onto a pickup truck, including our beds.

After we had a quick breakfast, prepared by one of our thoughtful neighbours, a Volkswagen minibus arrived. Mum, us four children, and our grandparents, all took our seats. A kind neighbour also accompanied us for moral support and to help in any way he could.

The minibus was also packed with boxes of fragile Delft-ware, and a pile of loose blankets was placed behind the long back seat, along the window. Hens and chickens were in tea chests, all well-ventilated, and, last but not least, Sally sat beside Ted and me, bemused by it all, while Toby was curled up under our seat. Pop didn't join us, as he had to drive the car.

Prompted by Mum, both Ted and I had one important task to do before we departed our beloved townland. Ted took Toby in his arms and we got out of the minibus and presented our amazing neighbour Danjoe with the late Mrs O'Brien's dog, the same little dog we'd fed and taken care of since her passing and who always waited with Sally at our farmyard gate to welcome us home each school day. Tears welled up in Danjoe's eyes, no doubt remembering the late Mrs O'Brien and the particular day he gave Toby to her when she first came to live in Gorse Valley.

All vehicles were lined up and ready to begin our long journey to County Dublin, with Pop's car at the rear. Tears flowed like a never-ending river as we bade our lovely neighbours of Gorse Valley a heart-wrenching farewell. Handkerchiefs were drawn across the eyes of all and sundry as they wished us well in our new life. They stood at the side of the road, waving us a last goodbye with their hands in the air. It was a heartbreaking time for both us and them. Some of our neighbours were elderly and it was possible that we would never see them again. The fact that Mrs O'Brien had passed on, and now we were leaving the small community of Gorse Valley, added to the sadness of the situation.

It was a tough time for Nano and Grandpa, leaving everyone and everything they had known throughout their lives behind. They still had relatives living nearby, including Grandpa's sister, our Grand Aunt Mary, and leaving them was one of the toughest decisions they'd had to make in their entire lives. As far as my grandparents were concerned, we may as well have been going to Australia, as County Dublin at that time seemed so far away.

This was also a tough time for Mum. Her brother, our uncle Bill, was suffering from ill health and had become immobile. The only one left to take care of him was a kind neighbour. Tears ran down Mum's face a few days before our move as she bade her brother an emotional goodbye.

En route, the old lorries rattled their way from town to town, with our VW minibus somewhere in the middle of the convoy. Our animals were scared to death by the motion and noise, and they mooed, bleated, neighed, and Neddy brayed.

We stopped a few times along the way to have tea and scones, which we had packed earlier to sustain us. It also gave us an opportunity to make sure the animals were okay in the lorries and to give them a drink of water. During our second stop, Pop took our raggedy white-haired goat Maisy out of one of the lorries and put her sitting on the back seat of his car. She was looking rather poorly, and he wasn't sure if she would survive the long journey to Dublin.

During our trip, I was not concerned about our new home and life in County Dublin. My main worry was about Neddy, as I feared he would fall out of the back of the lorry. Pop reassured me that he was following behind and that Neddy would be fine.

Six hours later, we arrived at our new farm holding to find our immediate new neighbours had dinner waiting for us. Luckily for us, Pop had informed them of the date we were arriving. Once we finished dinner, we unloaded our animals, and to say mayhem and madness ensued would be a total understatement.

Having been locked up in the lorries for such a long time, our livestock took flight. With their heads high and tails in the air, they ran to the far end of our new fields. We were thankful that our neighbours were on hand to help us, and we managed to get our animals under control and contained in their sheds. They were starving, so Pop and Grandpa fed and watered them, giving them extra helpings to calm them. Our goat survived and lived for a further eight months afterwards.

Here began a new life for all of us. For our parents and grandparents, this entailed a different way of farming and familiarising themselves with their surroundings and neighbours. For us children, it meant attending a new school and forming new friendships.

Anyone who ever moved from one location to another will know that being a new resident in a locality is difficult. It is like going into the unknown, and there is no way of telling what is in store for you. Your neighbours have no idea what kind of person or family have come to live amongst them and, likewise, you don't know them or their family.

But, where land is involved, that level of difficulty and anxiety is on a much higher level. Farmers, generally speaking and wherever they live, are covetous of their piece of land or property and don't take too kindly to strangers taking over what could be an extension of their patch. In our situation, there was no need for us to worry about this issue, as all of our immediate neighbours and those in our surrounding locality couldn't have been more helpful and supportive, and we appreciated their welcome and kindness.

The evening before we started attending our new school, Cait sat at the kitchen table biting her nails, Elizabeth was quieter than usual, and Ted was complaining of stomach aches. I sat beside Mum, on an armchair near our fire, with my arms firmly around her waist.

"Mum, I don't want to go to a new school tomorrow. I want to go back to my old school in Kerry." I said.

"Maggie, it's impossible now, darling. You cannot go back to your old school. But, you will like your new school and, you will have more friends to play with." She assured me.

Ted, our sisters and I often recalled our first day in our new school – it was like the beginning of our school years all over again. Mum and Pop accompanied us, to introduce us to our new teachers.

As we entered each of our new classrooms, the pupils gaped at us, as if we had come from another planet. Out in the play yard, some pupils jeered and called us culchies. Our thick Kerry brogue didn't help much but we survived. We soon found some nice friends, which helped to cushion the strangeness of it all. Being fluent speakers of the Irish language also helped, and having my big burly brother close by was always comforting for me.

In the years that followed, my brother and I, accompanied by Grandpa, enjoyed some short holidays in Gorse Valley, staying with relatives we had missed so much. When we stepped onboard that dark-green, multi-carriage train, bound for our old hometown, we were on cloud nine. I remember it well, with its mahogany doors and window frames, and long red velvet-cushioned seats. We were mesmerised as it huffed and puffed through the countryside in those bright summer days. Ted and I ticked off each station we stopped at in a notebook, all the while getting nearer to our final destination. And the lemonade and biscuits Grandpa bought from the sweet trolley was the highlight of our journey.

Ted and I soon renewed our acquaintance with some of our friends in Gorse Valley and we played together as if time and distance had never existed. We boasted a little about our lifestyle in County Dublin, about our new friends, our shiny new bikes, and our modern farm machinery. But our Kerry friends soon brought us back down to earth with a bang, slagging our thick Dublin accents, which we had slowly acquired.

Accompanied by Grandpa, we spent some time with Danjoe and Ada, recalling the great times we had spent together in the past. Spending quality time with Grand Aunt Mary was the highlight of our visits, as of course she was always uppermost in Grandpa's mind.

However, our visits to Gorse Valley were always tinged with a little sadness, as our former home was uninhabited and was beginning to fall into disrepair. But at least the farmlands, though they were of poor quality were being used by local farmers.

Our move to County Dublin was indeed life-changing and stressful, but, while we didn't appreciate it at the time, it was a positive and brave undertaking for our parents and grandparents. Our new farm holding was situated near all the modern amenities of the time, and bordered County Kildare. Ted and I had a better quality of life, as farm chores became easier with the use of modern machinery. We also had more time to play, and better access to shops and health care. As we got older, we had more opportunities for education, and when we left school, there were more career options.

It is difficult to put into words just how much I appreciate the sacrifices that my parents and grandparents made for me and my siblings. From humble beginnings, they worked hard to better themselves in life and, in turn, gave us a better future. But the shoreline where Ted and I frolicked in our childhood days and the rugged beauty of Gorse Valley, between the mountains and sea, will always hold a special place in my heart.

Brother

A person who is there
when you need him,
someone who picks you up
when you fall.
A person who takes your side
when no one else will.
My brother, Ted,
forever and always my friend.

– Maggie –

About Author

Mary M. Trant, a native of County Kerry, Ireland, has a deep connection to her rural roots, where she spent her early years within a tight knit farming community. For a child it was a place of unrestricted freedom and delight. However, a few years later a significant and life changing event, was the inspiration for this work of creative nonfiction.

In adult life and after taking a career break to focus on raising her children, Mary rediscovered her love for hand knitting. Since then, she has built a thriving business, creating high-end newborn baby outfits for professional photographers. Her exquisite creations have found homes across the globe, from the United Kingdom to the United States of America, New Zealand, and Australia.

Her debut book offers a captivating insight into some marvellous childhood adventures, while living between the mountains and the sea in Gorse Valley. Drawing on her intimate knowledge of rural life and lore, she weaves together tales of fairs, fairies and the Banshee in County Kerry, painting a vivid picture inspired by her early years.

Mary's unique blend of firsthand experiences and creative talent seamlessly come together to create masterfully written tales of wonderful childhood days – peppered with laughter, and some sad moments – with every turn of the page.

Acknowledgements

My gratitude to Eamon of Clear-View Fiction Editing. com who's knowledge of how a story needs to develop is extensive. He brings humour to the editing process and an expert in his craft.

It has been a pleasure to work with Teija Lammi at Reedsy.com, for my book cover design and interior design, who's work exceeds one hundred percent every time.

Thank you to Linda Clarke Photography.ie for my author photo and to Geraldine Shields – geraldine.shields at Instagram for my book cover photo. Two extremely talented Photographers in their respective specialities.

Thank you to Keenaghan Cottage.com and to Hickey Race Engineering (hreirl.com) for their continued support.

I will be forever grateful to Carol Trow at Reedsy.com, who meticulously proofread my book.

I sincerely thank Oonagh Charleton, Frances Preston, Giséle Poncelet, Bill Montiglio and Judith Hughes for Beta Reading a very raw first draft of my manuscript.

And indeed, thank you to anyone else who supported me in any way during this writing journey.

Mary

Printed in Great Britain
by Amazon

60633510R00129